Challenging Gifted Children

Leah Welte, M.A.

Teacher Created Materials, Inc.

Cover Design by Darlene Spivak

Made in U.S.A.

ISBN 1-55734-884-7

Order Number TCM 884

Table of Contents

Introduction

Since its inception, the education of gifted and able learners in the United States has been a roller coaster ride. Its high points have coincided with times of national concern such as that caused by Sputnik and its lows with the tightening of budgetary belts. In spite of this ebb and flow, some children with unusual potential have been nurtured, educated, and have made outstanding contributions as adults. However, there is no way to determine how many more youngsters with this innate ability might have reached their zeniths had a comprehensive, sequential, strongly supported, and appropriately funded educational program existed for them.

Children with high-level ability are found in every culture, age, and size and in your classroom. *Professional's Guide: Challenging Gifted Children* provides you with the concepts and successful practices for the effective education of these students. The chapters address such aspects as strategies for discovering which students are gifted, why they require special education—and what happens when they do not receive it, as well as suggested professional development for you. Methods for adapting commercial resources along with strategies for creating new materials are also included. Finally, ideas for you to help parents of gifted students guide their youngsters more effectively through the childhood maze are also presented. Throughout the chapters are practical examples and ideas which you can integrate into your existing curriculum and use to stimulate a single child, a small group of students, or an entire class of gifted youngsters. An extensive reference section enables you to pursue further information about any of the topics. Though founded on a theoretical base, the major focus of this book is to provide you with a pragmatic resource to increase your understanding and effectiveness in helping this country's greatest natural resource become our best national product.

Author's Note

I thankfully acknowledge the guidance and stimulation I have received over thirty years from wonderful mentors like Ruth Martinson, Jeanne Delp, Barbara Clark, and Sandra Kaplan. Also, I have used the term "she" to stand for the teacher and "he" for the student throughout the book to avoid the interruption and repetition of the use of he/she, realizing, of course, that fine male teachers of the gifted and bright female students are plentiful. Finally, I thank my family for their patience, understanding, and help during this stimulating writing process and those who were so willing to provide the feedback necessary to strengthen the quality of this book.

Who Are the Gifted, and How Are They Found?

A Brief History

Working on behalf of gifted youngsters requires patience and perseverance. The current arbitrary attitude of our American society toward these children is demonstrated on the school yard, in the teacher's lounge, and over the back fence. This conviction is not universally shared around the world nor has it been throughout history, and our nation neglects its intellect at its own peril.

The concept of giftedness had its beginnings in ancient times, perhaps with Plato's selection of unusual youngsters to train for later leadership positions, and each culture throughout the ages has established its own definition of what constitutes giftedness. Early in our own country's history, Thomas Jefferson proposed a legislative bill titled "The Diffusion of Education" to provide at public expense for the university education of promising American youths, specifically to prepare them for leadership roles in the New World (Hildreth, 1966). During the Industrial Revolution of the 1700s and again in the Sputnik era of the 1950s, it was the budding scientists and inventors who were sought out and sup-

Working on behalf of gifted youngsters requires patience and perseverance.

1

ported. Interspersed between these peaks of interest, there has been much emphasis upon the "melting pot" concept with sentiment against "elitism" and with equal rights becoming associated with homogeneity and conformity (Whitmore, 1980). In spite of the American values of excellence and innovation, middle-class standards have consistently promoted the practicality of the Protestant work ethic and the status quo. In fact, as recently as 1940, Carroll (1940) pointed out the truism that concerted effort is made to raise the slower child to the norm and simply by ignoring his needs, a less direct effort is made to pull down the gifted child to this same level. This phenomenon stems from the fact that we have persisted in misinterpreting the statement in our Declaration of Independence, "all men are created equal." The fact that this phrase suggests every person's right to an equally appropriate education rather than that all should receive the identical instruction has been lost upon our American society.

The current emphasis upon educating gifted youngsters, though intermittent, began in the 1960s, coinciding with the increased concern about world problems such as overpopulation, the cold war with its nuclear escalation, diminishing natural resources, and the need for advanced technology.

Prior to this century, any study of advanced intelligence consisted of the analysis of "genius" with mention made of brilliant inventors, remarkable scholars, and artists of exceptional talent. Child prodigies were described, such as Mozart who composed minuets before the age of four, sonatas at five, and a symphony at eight. Connections were made between genius and instability or even insanity, and gifted children were exhibited as though they were freaks in sideshows. Other highly gifted people went unrecognized by their teachers as in the case of Thomas Edison who was "too stupid to learn anything" and Albert Einstein who was "mentally slow, unsociable, and adrift forever in his foolish dreams." The advent of Terman (1916) and his studies of gifted children in the early 1900s brought about a more scientific understanding of exceptionality. Contrary to earlier myths, he found that his subjects were superior in all respects, i.e., physically larger and stronger, emotionally more stable, and socially adept, as well as intellectually advanced. In fact, he created his own myth—that gifted children were outstanding in every way, which enabled society to judge that they needed no particular support or encouragement. More recent studies have established that the gifted population may possess a wider variation of traits than others because of their spectrum of capabilities. Analysis of individual youngsters has revealed that although some may exhibit overall superi-

More recent studies have established that the gifted population may possess a wider variation of traits than others because of their spectrum of capabilities.

ority, others manifest their gift or talent in one area such as verbal, mathematical, mechanical ability, or a performing art talent with the others being less outstanding (Hildreth, 1966; Strang, 1960). Finally, it has been clearly established that gifted children do not readily become productive, successful adults without the appropriate guidance and education, and it has been estimated that anywhere from 15 to 50 percent become significant underachievers (Marland, 1972).

Notwithstanding the extensive research which has been done relative to giftedness, this population remains the most misunderstood and relatively unsupported educational group in American schools. Public attention has been consistently focused upon the culturally disadvantaged and physically or educationally challenged rather than the group which represents this nation's most valuable natural resource. It would appear consistent with historical fact to say that the gifted have been either largely ignored, or they have been exploited and pressured to perform for the public good rather than for their own personal satisfaction.

Determining who should be called gifted has been accomplished from a number of different perspectives.

Who Are the Gifted?

Determining who should be called gifted has been accomplished from a number of different perspectives. Initially, a relatively narrow view was held as when Terman chose for his study the top two percent of children taking a test of individual intelligence (Terman, 1925). By the 1940s and 1950s, Witty (1940) and Hildreth (1952) had recognized that personal and behavioral characteristics could be used as reliable indices and suggested that a profile of tested abilities and qualities be completed for individual children. Since that time, a number of well-known experts in gifted education have established broader concepts of giftedness. Guilford (1967) identified three major domains of intelligence—figural, symbolic, and semantic—and concluded that an excess of one or more of these constitutes giftedness. Renzulli (1977) substituted a production for an aptitude orientation when he introduced a novel triple Venn diagram model including above-average ability, task commitment, and creativity, the area at which these overlap producing giftedness. Gardner (1983) has proposed that an individual can be advanced in one or more of seven independent intelligences—verbal/linguistic, logical/mathematical, visual/spatial, bodily/kinesthetic, musical/rhythmic, interpersonal, and intrapersonal; whereas, Sternberg (1985) has theorized three types of giftedness—memory/analytic, synthetic/creative, and practical. Clark (1988, p. 7) has taken into account recent brain/mind research when formulating her definition which explains that "giftedness results from the advanced and accelerated integration of

3

functions within the brain expressed through abilities such as those involved in cognition, creativity, academic aptitude, leadership, or the visual and performing arts." Though the more recent theories share a common belief in the existence of an array of capabilities, it is clear that there is a variety of viewpoints regarding the particulars.

For practical purposes, the federal government established its own parameters in the landmark Marland definition (1972) and revised them in the Education Consolidation and Improvement Act (1981), both of which are listed below since they have characterized the program definitions in a majority of the states offering services for the gifted.

Gifted and talented children are those identified by professionally qualified persons who by virtue of outstanding abilities are capable of high performance.

Gifted and talented children are those identified by professionally qualified persons who by virtue of outstanding abilities are capable of high performance. These are children who require differentiated educational programs and services beyond those normally provided by the regular school program in order to realize their contribution to self and society.

Children capable of high performance include those with demonstrated achievement and/or potential ability in any of the following areas:

1. *General intellectual aptitude (usually determined using IQ and achievement tests)*

2. *Specific academic aptitude (usually in a single subject such as mathematics and determined using achievement scores)*

3. *Creative or productive thinking (often determined using tests of creativity—the most difficult group to serve consistently and appropriately in public education)*

4. *Leadership ability (some standardized questionnaires exist to help in identification—not a usual area of formal service)*

5. *Visual and performing arts (often determined by professionals in each field utilizing portfolios)* (Marland, 1972)

Gifted and talented children are those who give evidence of high performance capability in areas such as intellectual, creative, artistic, leadership capacity, or specific academic fields, and who require services or activities not ordinarily provided by the school in order to fully develop such capabilities (ECIA, Sec. 582).

How Are These Children Found?

A variety of identification tools have been employed in the process of determining which children possess the attributes defined as giftedness. The most proven, yet controversial, remains the individual test of intelligence or IQ test, the two most popular of which have been the Wechsler and the Stanford-Binet Scales. Less often, the Slosson Intelligence Test, a modified version of the Stanford-Binet, and the Kaufman Assessment Battery for Children (K-ABC) have been used. The Stanford-Binet and Slosson scales yield a single general intelligence score and a mental age based heavily upon verbal abilities. The Wechsler (WPSSI, WISC, WAIS) is more illuminating for us because it provides, as shown in the sample below, separate scores for verbal and performance abilities, derived from scaled scores (1–19) on six subtests in each area as well as an overall IQ score. It is clear from examining the list that the mental functions most completely sampled are short-term and long-term memory, associations, and convergent reasoning. The two least frequently involved are divergent reasoning and evaluation. Though there is no expected profile for gifted students (Wilkinson, 1993), similarities, vocabulary, and block design are the most significant subtests when determining giftedness. IQ tests do measure much of what we consider to be necessary to current academic success, and this information can be used in helping to plan a more meaningful educational program for individual students.

Wechsler Intelligence Scale for Children (WISC-III)

Verbal

- ◆ Information—collection of knowledge; curiosity; alertness to world
- ◆ Similarities—logical abstract reasoning; ability to associate ideas
- ◆ Arithmetic—numerical reasoning and speed of numerical manipulation
- ◆ Vocabulary—language usage and accumulated verbal learning ability
- ◆ Comprehension—practical social judgment; common sense
- ◆ Digit Span—short-term memory; concentration and attention

Total Score = Verbal IQ

Performance

♦ Picture Completion—awareness of environmental detail; visual acuity

♦ Picture Arrangement—ability to understand interpersonal situations

♦ Block Design—visual-motor-spatial coordination; concentration; effort

♦ Object Assembly—manipulative and perceptual speed; synthesis

♦ Coding—visual-motor speed and coordination; short-term memory

♦ Mazes—planning ability or foresight; perceptual organization

Total Score = Performance IQ

Verbal IQ and Performance IQ = Full Scale IQ

A full-scale score of 100 is at the 50th percentile while that of 130 corresponds to the 98th percentile (very superior range) and is often used as one indicator for placement in a program for students with general intellectual aptitude, i.e., intellectual giftedness. The data are different for individual students; however, general behaviors during the testing and patterns of scores can be predictive of the performance different types of children will exhibit in the classroom, as a review of the profiles for the representative students, Susan, Bart, Maria, and Roger, will exemplify.

Susan's scores on the Similarities and Vocabulary verbal subtests, the two most significant when testing for giftedness, were 19 and 18, (very superior level) while the others ranged from 14 through 16 (superior level), and her total verbal IQ was 138. Her scaled scores for performance were also relatively consistent, ranging from a 17 in Block Design, the most enlightening for establishing giftedness, to a 13, resulting in a performance IQ of 136. Her total IQ score was 140, the 99.6th percentile or highly-gifted range. The examiner noted that Susan was extremely anxious to please and sought to continue her answers even after she had been told that she had done very well. She appeared to be nervous both at the beginning of the examination period and at its finish.

Bart's profile indicated that he, too, exhibited rather even development in the areas examined, with his most common subtest scores ranging from 14 through 16 in both the verbal and performance areas. His verbal score was 133 and performance was 131 with the full-scale score of 132, the 98+ percentile. The psychologist indicated that he remained calm and focused during the entire test procedure and seemed to enjoy the experience.

Maria's verbal score of 124 was balanced by a higher performance score of 135, earning her a full-scale score of 131, the 98th percentile. The examiner stated that she came from a home where English was not the primary language, which could partially explain the somewhat depressed verbal score. Mention was also made of her enthusiasm to persevere on the test activities even after errors indicated that she might be reaching the ceiling of her ability.

Roger's verbal subtest scores revealed a significant range from a below average 9 in Digit Span to a 19 in Similarities, creating significant peaks and valleys when graphed, but yielding an impressive 148 as his verbal IQ score. His performance scores were all in the average range with a performance IQ of 112 and a total IQ score of 134. He was described as a complex subject who had to be urged and questioned further throughout the test in order to perform to his full capability.

All four of these students are considered gifted, but each will present a different challenge educationally. Susan represents the perfectionist child who will require special guidance emotionally together with a highly advanced intellectual challenge; whereas, Bart will endure, though not thrive, under any set of circumstances. Maria needs a modified language arts program along with rigorous activities in the visual and perceptual areas, while Roger is likely to experience great difficulty succeeding in school because of his uneven development and his apparently negative attitude. In each subsequent chapter, these four intellectually gifted youngsters will be discussed relative to their specific topics to help you envision how you can apply those principles to each gifted child in your classroom.

The scores on the Wechsler scales do not exceed 160, the 99.9+ percentile, while those of the Stanford-Binet can reach 180 and beyond. Students are estimated to exist among the general school population in the frequency (perhaps, more appropriately, the infrequency) listed below when using the Stanford-Binet scale:

All four of these students are considered gifted, but each will present a different challenge educationally.

7

IQ Level	Number of Pupils
130	3 per 100
137	1 per 100
150	1 per 1000
160	1 per 10,000
170	1 per 100,000
180	1 per 1,000,000

Tannenbaum (1994, p. 8) recently stated that "IQ instruments are valid and useful in measuring some of the most vital aspects of intelligence" even though "IQ bashing has been popular and widespread," especially because of the "supportive evidence that some minority groups are short-changed by scores that appear unfairly deflated."

Despite its imperfections, the IQ is as predictive of success in the early school years as any other measure and has an enviable seventy-year track record which no other instrument possesses.

Despite its imperfections, the IQ is as predictive of success in the early school years as any other measure and has an enviable seventy-year track record which no other instrument possesses. The IQ score gives some indication of the current mental level of that child in comparison with his own age group, and it makes a prediction as to the rate of that individual's growth in the future. The test performance has the advantage of being independent of reading and writing, and, therefore, is less reflective of school learning, identifying children with potential who may not yet be exhibiting it in their schoolwork. However, it has been recognized that there are other contributors to the overall intelligence of a child which can include special aptitudes, non-intellectual factors, and environmental influences. This knowledge, coupled with the fact that it is an expensive and time-consuming procedure administered individually by a trained psychologist or psychometrist, has brought about the development of other identification tools for use in conjunction with, or replacement of, the individual IQ test.

Other Tests of Ability or Achievement

One of the oldest and most respected set of tests that measure creativity, the mental function sparsely sampled by IQ tests, is the Torrance Tests of Creative Thinking (Torrance, 1966) which yields scores for fluency, flexibility, originality, and elaboration and exists in both verbal and figural forms. Achievement tests of the type commonly used by our school districts are frequently examined or administered in an effort to obtain a broader picture of a child's production. They typically test reading, language, and mathematics skills and knowledge in areas such as social studies and science, yielding percentile scores according to a child's comparison with his age group. The Raven's Progressive Matrices Test, the

Test of Nonverbal Intelligence (TONI), and the Abbreviated Binet for Disadvantaged (ABDA) have been employed to screen or identify culturally diverse students. Alternative tests that are used for screening or helping to identify very young children are the Peabody Picture Vocabulary Test, the Wide Range Achievement Test (WRAT), the Primary Mental Abilities Test and the Verbal Opposites Test (kindergarten and below). In later grades, group-administered tests such as the California Test of Mental Maturity (CTMM), the Lorge-Thorndike Intelligence Test, the Otis-Lennon Mental Ability Test, the Structure of Intellect Test (SOI), or the Developing Cognitive Abilities Test (DCAT) are more frequently used. Finally, the Scholastic Aptitude Test (SAT), commonly required as a college entrance exam, has been used successfully as early as grade six to identify students with unusual abilities in such areas as mathematics and language. Unfortunately, these tests do not as accurately identify all gifted students because they rely on skills in reading and following directions, resembling achievement tests in many ways.

The broadest defensible definition of giftedness should be used.

Principles of Identification

Identification for the purpose of placement in a gifted program is best accomplished by the preparation and evaluation of a case study with anecdotal information from the parent and involving a group of professionals representing various areas of expertise to include the teacher, principal, psychologist, counselor, and supervisor of the gifted program. The six principles below, to which my explanations have been added in italics, should underlie all identification procedures according to a national panel:

◆ **Advocacy**—Identification should be designed in the best interests of all students. *Procedures must be equitable and fair to all.*

◆ **Defensibility**—Procedures should be based on the best available research and recommendations. *Updated information is available from groups such as the National Research Center on the Gifted and Talented at the University of Connecticut.*

◆ **Equity**—Procedures should guarantee that no one is overlooked. The civil rights of students should be protected. Strategies should be outlined for identifying the disadvantaged gifted. *This has been a highly emphasized focus area in many states.*

◆ **Pluralism**—The broadest defensible definition of giftedness should be used. *As many types of gifted students should be identified and served as is feasible.*

9

- **Comprehensiveness**—As many as possible gifted learners should be identified and served. *An aggressive search should enable the largest number of students to receive attention.*

- **Pragmatism**—Whenever possible, procedures should allow for the modification and use of tools and resources on hand. *Tests, procedures, etc., already established should be used to maximize efficiency and minimize cost.*

Concluding Remarks

A successful screening and identification program requires early identification and consistent nurturing of gifted students in order to prevent undesirable behavior patterns such as underachievement, social alienation, and emotional disturbance. In addition, the search must be continual as they do not always evidence the obviously remarkable performance of a Mozart which can be recognized by casual observation without the benefit of formal measurements. The children we call gifted do not possess characteristics foreign to all other children. However, the fact that they exhibit these characteristics at an earlier age, to a greater degree, and in a different combination, sets them apart and necessitates consistent challenge so that those qualities can flourish. Employing elaborate measures to locate and label these youngsters is meaningless if their learning experiences are not changed appropriately. Therefore, in order to determine how to educate your gifted students, you must become aware of the uniqueness that these children possess, which is the goal of the next chapter.

The children we call gifted do not possess characteristics foreign to all other children.

What Are the Unique
Needs of Gifted Children?

Overview

Through experience and research about giftedness and temperament, I have recognized general traits which characterize gifted children as a group and the variations which are more dependent upon their personalities. Although they possess as many, if not more, differences than any sample of students drawn from an average population, this information does provide a backdrop against which you can evaluate individuals. Lists of qualities abound, and you can examine the detailed organizational patterns developed by Clark (1988) in five domains, Gardner (1983) describing the seven intelligences, and several others by reviewing their books listed in the reference section. Moreover, an understanding of the temperaments or personality types of gifted youngsters is an important factor which is discussed in depth by Myers & Myers (1980) and Lawrence (1987). The information presented here can be used as a guide in the creation or choice of learning experiences for your gifted students as well as in your daily interactions with them. It also has often proven of value when shared at Back to School Nights, during parent conferences, and with other teachers.

The information presented here can be used as a guide in the creation or choice of learning experiences for your gifted students as well as in your daily interactions with them.

11

General Traits of Gifted Children

◆ A curiosity and desire to learn are the greatest allies in initially motivating and promoting sustained involvement in a wide variety of advanced studies.

◆ A long attention span and need to delve deeply into a subject suggest that class periods and duration of units should be of sufficient length that satisfaction is felt at their culmination.

◆ A resistance to routine and drill indicates that creative strategies and fewer lessons with fewer application problems should be devoted to the mastery of such mundane but significant topics as multiplication facts or states and capitals.

◆ A desire to question, express ideas, and receive a reaction leads to lively and intense discussions where the adult is often not seen as the sole authority and should not perceive that argumentation is the desire.

◆ An interest in exploring topics beyond the chronological age and maturity level results in the challenge of locating resources at an appropriate reading and comprehension level, as well as the need to provide time for guided independent study. Adherence to regular grade level requirements and materials is inappropriate, and access to more advanced materials must be encouraged.

◆ An intense sensitivity to fair play, honor, and truth makes it necessary to carefully think out your actions and interactions with individual students so that a relationship of trust is maintained. Fostering the development of heroes and the pursuit of justice should be balanced with the development of the understanding that life and individuals cannot always be perfectly fair or honest.

◆ An ability to think at advanced levels of complexity dictates that the curriculum at all levels must include activities and discussions of concepts such as cause-effect, alike-different, "trees-forest," and cross-curricular relationships which promote a fabric of integrated learning.

◆ An advanced sense of humor allows you to employ this strategy in your relationships with even young gifted students; however, this may also cause distractions by using humor as a means of seeking attention.

A curiosity and desire to learn are the greatest allies in initially motivating and promoting sustained involvement in a wide variety of advanced studies.

♦ A need to interact with mental peers leads to relationships with age-peers through gifted programs, older-aged friends, teachers, and other adults and often necessitates an arbitrary grouping in the school setting.

♦ A high level of verbal ability and language development may be evidenced in discussions between individuals, as well as with small and large groups but should not be misinterpreted as arrogance in one so young.

♦ To possess areas of great ability enables outstanding accomplishments and intense interests along with some of lesser strength, which can result in avoidance, frustration, or the need for appropriate reinforcement in learning the concepts.

♦ To disregard the need for social and physical development or exercise in favor of intellectual pursuits can result in health problems, obesity, or social difficulties if not adequately addressed in the educational program.

♦ To process ideas very rapidly, almost without being aware of the steps involved, can cause difficulty if you demand in all cases that every step be demonstrated; for example, in the number strand of mathematics.

An area of importance which I believe largely accounts for the variety in gifted youngsters is that of personality type and learning style.

Personality Types and Learning Styles

An area of importance which I believe largely accounts for the variety in gifted youngsters is that of personality type and learning style. Human behavior is not random but rather occurs in patterns according to mental habits which Jung (1933) called psychological types. Jung and his followers postulated that one's personality type is deeply ingrained and can be modified but not markedly changed. Based upon his original work, Myers and Myers (1980) developed sixteen personality types which have been characterized as combinations created from these four major categories:

extroversion (E) v. introversion (I)
a preference for the outer world of people and things
a preference for the inner world of idea and thought
sensing (S) v. intuition (N)
attention to facts and details from experience via the five senses
attention to possibilities; the big picture by means of a sixth sense

13

thinking (T) v. feeling (F)
decisions based on cause and effect, justice and fair play
decisions utilizing personal values and need for harmony
judging (J) v. perceiving (P)
planned, organized way with control and order
remaining flexible and spontaneous with unexpected and
unplanned occurrences

A number of studies of learning styles in the gifted have indicated that these youngsters from grades four through twelve dislike drill, recitation, and lectures and prefer options, independent study, and nonconformity. In addition, one study of gifted adolescents found that nearly two thirds of that population was evenly divided between extroversion and introversion and thinking and feeling, but that the group was largely intuitive and perceiving (Alvino, 1989).

My classroom experiences with gifted youngsters confirm that it is important to incorporate psychological-type theory into your thinking so that you can facilitate the development of preferred methods of learning, as well as exercise the modes they would rather avoid. The common qualities of gifted children are evidenced in all my students since they enjoy thinking about ideas and their meaning, thrive when avenues of thought are explored, and are motivated when variety and experiences involving depth of learning are provided (N). On the other hand, a primary variation occurs between the youngsters who are enthused when I provide them wide parameters and a choice of activities (P) and those who have the desire to know in detail what is expected by me for a particular project (J). Another exists between the children who thrive upon sharing their ideas aloud and gravitate toward group experiences or projects (E) and those who are content simply to listen in groups and prefer to work alone (I). The final major difference appears between the students who are impatient, critical with themselves and others, and possess the need to be in control (T) and those who are highly cooperative, compliant, and consistently seek to accommodate others' needs before their own (F).

While all children possess each temperamental quality to some degree, the resolute perceiving child in my class can ponder his choices so long that the quality beginning of his project is left unfinished, is done in a frenzy at the last moment, or is turned in late. Conversely, the extremely judging child can be in such a hurry to finish a project that the quality and depth of thought are insufficient or missing altogether. The intensely introverted child finds it very difficult to enter effectively into our discussions or group

> The intensely introverted child finds it very difficult to enter effectively into our discussions or group activities.

activities. On the other hand, the high-powered extroverted child's challenge is to modify his enthusiasm for sharing his ideas and his desire for control so that others may have equal opportunity. It is important that you endeavor to help each of your students develop an adequate balance while their personalities are still emerging.

The students, Susan, Bart, Maria, and Roger, introduced in Chapter 1 are composites of those in my classes over the years. They personalize the general profiles of gifted youngsters yet demonstrate the variety of their needs.

> **Susan** is a highly gifted girl who takes her studies, and her life, extremely seriously. She evidences a high degree of interest and motivation toward the topics introduced in class and spends many hours on her homework. This young lady's fast-paced thought and piercing comments motivate me and her peers to approach discussions with her only when adequately prepared. Her personality type is INTJ (Introvert, Intuitive, Thinking, Judging), which causes her to enjoy working alone, strongly resist participation in group projects, and to have an understanding of many topics and people beyond her years. Moreover, her strong thinking and judgmental disposition result in a difficulty in tolerating sloppiness of any sort, not to mention an impatience with the silly behavior of her less precocious peers. She is equally self-critical, however, with the highest expectations reserved for herself.

> **Bart,** an ISTJ (Introvert, Sensing, Thinking, Judging), seems almost to be a stoic, so poised and self-controlled. Though he evidences a strong need to progress in learning, his advanced maturity and strong moral sense enable him to generate his own enrichment activities with a minimum of fuss. His abilities appear to be equally well developed as evidenced by his fine accomplishments in swim meets, at the piano, and in his studies. During discussions his occasional comments, made only when called on by me, are often enlightening, with his advanced vocabulary making it reminiscent of a friendly sparring between adults. On topics of interest, he is willing and able to pursue research over an extended period with little supervision, though he does not yet create a product that is commensurate with his ability.

> **Maria** is the vivacious, outgoing girl commonly noted in an ENFP (Extrovert, Intuitive, Feeling, Perceiving). She is

It is important that you endeavor to help each of your students develop an adequate balance while their personalities are still emerging.

15

helpful to all and enthusiastically provides the positive leadership necessary to succeed in group work. This champion of the underdog seems to know the appropriate statements to facilitate the resolution of difficulties among her friends. Her highly sensitive nature and gentle, though perceptive, sense of humor make others listen carefully to her comments during class discussions, even though her vocabulary is not as advanced as some of her peers. She is comfortable in working on a number of projects at one time and is satisfied when she has completed what she believes is a good job. Though it may be at the last moment or is sometimes missing when grading time arrives, she is apologetic and eventually turns in the product if reminded.

Special attention must be given to creating an atmosphere of exploration and discovery.

Roger is the bane of his peers' and my existence with his INFP (Introvert, Intuitive, Feeling, Perceiving) nature. He is highly verbal with thoughts constantly tumbling through his mind and very often from his mouth. His sharp wit and impish inclination cause him to send verbal boomerangs into a serious lesson, resulting in the expected reaction from me. He is intensely interested in computer programming and cartooning, topics which are, at best, tangential to our regular curriculum. His involvement in school work is occasional, and he would rather read his current science fiction story or draw his favorite cartoon character (literally, if possible, or figuratively in his daydreams). When a curricular topic does excite his interest, he is not content to complete the task as outlined but does it his way—or not at all.

Concluding Remarks

Information about the four major temperaments and qualities of gifted youngsters should be considered when planning curriculum. Special attention must be given to creating an atmosphere of exploration and discovery. Opportunities for individual research projects across the curriculum and a degree of academic freedom and variation with regard to the pace, process, and product are also necessary. In order to accommodate their specific and varied needs, you must be flexible in your reactions to your students. Some will respond best when they note your approval, while others desire your recognition. Another group values most your appreciation for their accuracy, whereas their counterparts want to be acknowledged for their cleverness. Using your knowledge and intuition will enable you to succeed with the mainstream. However, some gifted children exhibit greater complexity due to unusual hereditary or environmental conditions and require more individualized strategies, the subject of the next chapter.

What About the Struggling Gifted Child?

Challenging Gifted Students

Too often gifted youngsters will be assigned to your class who present additional challenges because they are struggling in some respect. Through research on the causes and working with various students over the years, I have developed techniques that can help increase your effectiveness in helping these children achieve in your program. Again, please keep in mind the uniqueness of each individual as you read about an underachieving, learning disabled, adolescent girl, and highly perfectionistic, culturally diverse, or economically disadvantaged gifted youngsters.

Underachieving and Learning Disabled Gifted

Among the most misunderstood and maligned gifted children are those who historically have been labeled as underachieving. This misnomer has been applied because the practitioners observed that they possessed high capability but were not performing success-fully in school, based upon achievement test scores or grades or both. An additional dimension—a slight learning disability—often is also present in these children. You will find two basic

> Among the most misunderstood and maligned gifted children are those who historically have been labeled as underachieving.

17

groups—those who are aggressive and act out and those who withdraw and waste away. Both types represent highly frustrating, complex, and often baffling challenges to their parents and you. Conversely, successfully solving this problem with a high-potential child is one of the greatest achievements and highest rewards you will gain from your interaction with gifted children and their parents.

Characteristics of Underachievers and Learning Disabled

From observation of children and a review of the studies and projects (Karnes, 1986; Whitmore, 1980 & 1986; Rimm, 1986), I have noted a number of characteristics peculiar to underachievers. Though the entire list does not appear in any particular child, a pattern of these negative behaviors becomes evident when observing him over an extended period of time. Since the child has developed the syndrome from an early age, to change it requires patience, understanding, and the implementation of several strategies which will be explored in detail later in this chapter.

> **Though the entire list does not appear in any particular child, a pattern of these negative behaviors becomes evident when observing him over an extended period of time.**

◆ Low self-esteem; negative self-evaluation; manipulation of adults and peers—often, these feelings are masked by bravado, appearing to be a superior attitude. One significant adult may be played against the other, for example, teacher v. parent or ex-husband v. ex-wife. The support of all significant adults is necessary to change this.

◆ Rebellious; moody; bossy; easily angered or lonely and withdrawn—this behavior is a direct outgrowth of his feeling a lack of self-worth and requires time, repeated debriefing about situations, and patience.

◆ Lack of self-discipline; feeling of helplessness resulting in lack of responsibility for actions—because he believes that he has little or no control over his present conditions, he is not accountable. Creating a desire to seek classroom responsibility and rewarding with specific praise for small successes can change this.

◆ Procrastination; poor study habits; lack of, or spotty development of, academic skills—difficulty in focusing attention and not actively listening causes gaps in learning. A daily/weekly behavior contract and tutoring by an adult are often effective.

◆ Lack of persistence; rationalization of difficulties; little motivation for academic achievement—fear of failure causes him not to try, i.e., if I risk nothing, I lose nothing. A string of small successes in studies must occur to help him prove himself.

◆ Nebulous or no future goals—educational, personal, or job-related—the belief that he has little power to control his life is coupled with the fact that no connection has been made between what he accomplishes today and his long-term achievement. Goal-setting discussions, modeling by adults about their thought processes, and involvement with other gifted friends who have these goals is important.

◆ No outside interest or hobby or exclusive interest in one or two areas—usually, if an area exists, success is easily achieved with the possibility of failure remote. Beginning with the existing interest is important.

◆ Resistance to influence from teacher or parent; perceived rejection from these adults—these are the adults who he believes keep control away from him. Interactions with a teacher-child-parent evaluated daily-weekly behavior contract can help to alter this.

◆ Poor leadership ability; dislike of competition—again, there are the fears of failure and rejection by others. Even a degree of success in classroom leadership opportunities and assignments can change this.

◆ Prone to fantasize; complain of boredom—these are often diversionary tactics to avoid the real issue. Making sure that learning activities are, in fact, appropriately challenging and then holding him to their completion through the behavior contract is a key to altering this behavior.

◆ Negative attitude toward school and teachers; choice of friends with like attitudes—it is difficult to like a place and those who are a constant reminder of his failure to produce or succeed, especially if he is unworthy in his own eyes. Become a genuine supporter with specific praise when you "catch him being good" and involve him consistently in group work with helpful student role models.

◆ Disorganization; daydreaming; chronic inattentiveness; under- or overly-involved in reading—Reading is an escape for the introverted, intuitive personality type and a burden for the sensing, extroverted type. The other habits provide a logical excuse for failure. These blocks to success can be brought under control when included in the behavior contract.

19

◆ A significant discrepancy between ability and achievement or between areas of achievement—the scores on the Wechsler test reveal peaks and valleys which may be only relative or may actually indicate a disability. Most often the indicators are poor spelling and handwriting, weak math or reading skills, or problems with auditory, motor, or visual perception. Usually the areas of weakness are avoided by him unless remedial or coping strategies are effected.

Causes of Underachievement

Gifted underachievers have originally chosen this behavior because it served them better than working to achieve. The responses become so ingrained that even when they make the decision to change, it takes time and effort to achieve. Though the learning disabled gifted child may not have chosen his circumstances, the situation generally becomes similar. Understanding the causes is the first step you must take to facilitate the necessary changes.

Home Factors

One explanation for children failing to achieve can be found from examining early family interactions. The problem is one of control and involves either the child dominating his parents or his overdependence on one or both of them. Early health problems can cause an initially positive mutual dependence between parent (usually mother) and child to become a hopelessly demanding and negative situation. Delays in fine motor or perceptual development may be inappropriately attributed to slower maturation rather than a disability to be treated in its early stage. Difficult sibling combinations such as like-sex children close in age, a highly gifted older child, or being the youngest child in a large family with older children can affect a gifted child. A sibling with a serious mental or physical challenge can also set the stage. Marital problems such as broken marriages with young bright children, the child born out of wedlock, or power struggles between parents and within the family also have the potential of resulting in the underachievement of a gifted child.

Personal Factors

Furthermore, a number of the qualities of giftedness can cause a child not to fulfill his capability. Internal pressures such as supersensitivity to criticism, unusually high expectations of self or others, or negative peer reaction can cause enough stress for the child to decide that achievement is not worth it (Whitmore, 1981).

Gifted underachievers have originally chosen this behavior because it served them better than working to achieve.

Moreover, the avoidance of perceived failure, an aspect of perfectionism, can result in his engaging only in activities for which success is virtually guaranteed (Adderholdt-Elliot, 1987). It is very possible that the discrepancy between what the child envisions with his advanced thinking ability and what he is capable of producing at an early age, especially if he is developmentally delayed or disabled, begins his sense of frustration and dissatisfaction with his achievement. On the other hand, a lack of social skills may cause the child to become associated with a peer group which dictates passive behavior or nonconformity in the classroom. Finally, he may become so immersed in a passionate interest or hobby, or have such deep interests in non-school topics, that the regular subjects are too restrictive and the curriculum too boring. It is interesting to note that studies have found, at minimum, a two-to-one ratio of boys to girls being reported as underachievers. I believe that this has resulted from the differing past expectations of society for males and females. From my observation of these children over the past thirty years, an increasing incidence of underperforming girls indicates that the gender gap may be closing.

It is interesting to note that studies have found, at minimum, a two-to-one ratio of boys to girls being reported as underachievers.

A brief description of Roger, our underachieving example, will help to crystallize the type of circumstances which explain this syndrome. His remedial plan is described in a later section of this chapter.

> **Roger** experienced severe asthma as a small child and spent many hours at the emergency center and in bed. His mother and father feared for his life and, therefore, were careful not to place many demands upon him. His mother read, played, and talked with him for hours on end to while away the sedentary time. At an early age, a laptop computer became his companion, rather than other children, along with the latest art materials in which he had evidenced interest. Though he entered kindergarten at the appropriate age, the fact that he was reading at a third-grade level and could operate a computer better than his teacher made him an anomaly to her and the other children. His chronic absences both frustrated her efforts at providing the necessary social interventions and absolved her of the need to challenge his intellect in a consistent manner. By the second grade, Roger's asthma attacks were nearly a thing of the past, and he was tested and qualified as a gifted student. His placement in a class with several other bright students at his home school was expedient, due to his mother's return to her career, but was ineffective in stimulating his intellect

throughout the day. At the end of grade four, it was decided that he would transfer to my school to join my full-time class of gifted children. Both of his parents, as well as Roger, realize that he needs to gain independence, learn to be more effective in his peer relationships, and perform better in his school subjects but they don't know how to achieve this.

School Factors

Though the seeds of underachievement are usually sprouted in the home, schools play a critical role in eliminating or intensifying this problem. By providing an appropriate environment from the beginning of his schooling, this difficulty stands the best chance of being modified. Since reality dictates that this often does not happen in the early years, the problem worsens and requires more extreme measures.

School Prevention or Remediation

The classroom setting which is most successful for all gifted youngsters is one in which there is neither too much rigidity where a power struggle ensues and social competition wherein failure is likely nor a laissez faire attitude in which disorganization can occur. Moderation involving a reasonable amount of flexibility, choice, and individualization, together with an emphasis on organization and time management is the appropriate structure. In my classroom of gifted students, the same vocabulary, attitude, and respect that I use with adults is accorded to each student. Challenging units are implemented that have specific requirements but are also somewhat open-ended and require self-responsibility. The students for whom this structure is difficult are presented the same challenge as those who are fully functioning, but support and guidance from their more responsible peers are built in through a Junior-Senior Partner relationship established at the beginning of the year. The chronic underachiever does experience initial failure to organize his resources and to manage his time effectively. When this happens during the first weeks, I counsel him and provide specific points of praise together with constructive criticism both in writing on projects and orally. If this technique is not sufficient to promote marked improvement after several weeks, I meet with him and his parents to discuss the problem and suggest a behavior contract.

You can neither be too concerned for the child, excusing and enabling his behaviors, nor too negative, reprimanding and punishing him in front of his classmates. A firm, fair, business-like attitude with genuine respect for the individual and faith in his abili-

You can neither be too concerned for the child, excusing and enabling his behaviors, nor too negative, reprimanding and punishing him in front of his classmates.

ty to succeed creates a positive climate in which change can occur. For example, during my underachiever's conference, I mention that each of us could profit from a similar behavior contract to effect a change in one of our less productive behaviors. The child is told that the final decision is his at this point, but that this is his opportunity to gain control in his areas of difficulty with our support. Usually these conditions appear to be favorable enough for him to choose to participate. He and his parents must determine what consequences will result from successes and failures as determined by the total point count for the day and week. It is his contract which he must bring to me and with which he evaluates his day with my guidance. His parents are told that their faithfulness in helping him implement the consequences will determine the contract's effectiveness. The initial scores on the behavior contract are characteristically lower, and the youngster usually forgets to bring it to me before the closing bell (equivalent to a 0 score) at least once or twice. Within several weeks, however, successful behaviors begin to appear with increasing frequency, and he discovers that there is a positive relationship between effort and the success which brings a sense of empowerment and personal satisfaction. He is still required to complete the same projects as his classmates and steadily increases his ability to manage these successfully. Encouragement, guidance, patience, and genuine and specific praise (and sometimes, reorganization and auto-correction, when setbacks occur) are critical to facilitate the process. The duration of this modification program should be dictated by the severity of his difficulty and his rate of progress. It is important that the youngster has the opportunity to experience several weeks before the year's end without the contract so that the confidence is gained that he can succeed on his own.

The single, most important intervention for an underachieving elementary child is to help him develop a healthy self-concept. Evidence from a number of studies indicates that self-concept and school achievement directly influence one another and that the underachiever possesses lower self-esteem than his achieving counterpart (Purkey, 1970). Therefore, this child must experience authentic, academic success acknowledged by his peers often enough to raise his estimation of himself. In point of fact, the underachiever's placement in a class of gifted students results in much greater gains than attempting to address his needs in the regular classroom, which Roger's example demonstrates.

> I have conducted an assessment of **Roger's** reading, language, and math skills, identifying several areas of deficiency. Though his verbal abilities far surpass his nonverbal

The single, most important intervention for an underachieving elementary child is to help him develop a healthy self-concept.

ones, he does not evidence a learning disability. I have met with his parents and him to present these findings, together with my documented description of his behavior and interactions with others in the classroom. Facilitating a discussion of his areas of strength, as well as need, and opportunities for empowerment in my classroom, I have offered a daily behavior contract for Roger's consideration. I have described it as a means for him to change his own behavior with the consistent, defined support from his parents and me. Roger has decided to give it a try, and he and his parents have determined what will constitute his rewards on days and weeks when he has reached sufficient success, as well as the consequences when he has not. The three specific goals in the areas of organization, paying attention, and turning in work on time have proven to be easily monitored by Roger. I have also encouraged him to use his word processing skill to produce his work via the computer and have indicated that he may wish to apply his artistic ability in the completion of the required products which already allow a degree of choice within each unit of study. Roger has had two intermittent weeks of low scores on his contract, has forgotten to initiate its completion once, and has suffered the consequences. In between these periods of lapse, he has shown that he does indeed desire to change by implementing the established behaviors and achieving the agreed upon rewards for six weeks. I have been very careful to refrain from actions which would enable Roger to manipulate the established procedure and seek opportunities to make specific and genuine positive comments about his progress in front of his peers whenever possible. They are beginning to seek his involvement in group activities particularly valuing his expertise in drawing and computer technology. Occasionally, I ask him what he thinks about the contract process and his progress; his comments indicate a definite improvement in his self-esteem and the degree to which he believes he can control his world. I comment that I have noticed him standing taller and responding with greater conviction. Though I caution that the contract is a crutch to give up at some point, Roger wants it maintained for the present.

The early years of life are the most critical in forming his opinion of himself.

Home Remediation

A large body of research with children at all age levels has indicated that the child's view of himself is based upon the way in which his significant others see him and is the primary force in his achievement. The early years of life are the most critical in forming his opinion of himself. The way he is treated molds the child, and there is little room for doubt that parents play an extremely vital role in the development of self-regard continuing into the adolescent years. Therefore, it is a fact that for a body of children, the predisposition to underachieve is present before they enter school, and the primary persons who must address this problem are the child's parents. The critical factor in developing high self-esteem is how the child interprets his parents' view of him rather than the amount of punishment, time spent with them, his physical attractiveness, income, or even social class or ethnic background (Purkey, 1970). It is of the greatest importance that you communicate to parents of underachievers that they must analyze and alter any detrimental attitudes portrayed to their children. The principles below can guide you and your student's parents.

◆ Provide a message to the child regarding what the expectations are for him with regard to school effort and achievement. His personal best effort, rather than perfection, should be the desire and that varies from day to day as well as from one subject to another, due to physical, social, or emotional factors.

◆ Encourage the child toward achievement and self-confidence by allowing him to struggle to a reasonable degree in the accomplishment of his own work. The persistence and perseverance gained from this effort are most important, as is the self-confidence which accompanies earned success. If it becomes necessary along the way to provide some assistance, be sure that this is given in a consistently decreasing manner until the dependency is finally extinguished.

◆ Make every attempt to maintain a calm, objective attitude, neither decreasing nor increasing the amount of attention, guidance, affection, freedom, and reaction to his success or failure than seem clearly necessary to a particular child.

◆ Work closely with the child to help him feel increasingly empowered to make decisions and to control his life as the necessary maturity and responsibility are demonstrated. Having him track his progress through graphing, scrapbooks of work, etc., can enable him to see clearly that he is improving measurably.

◆ Maintain a strong alliance with the child's remaining significant others, neither discussing him in his presence nor allowing him to drive a wedge between one adult and another.

Provide a clear message to the child regarding what the expectations are for him with regard to school effort and achievement.

- Help the child perceive any failure as a step along the road to success from which strength and experience are gained. Healthy competition needs to be viewed as a positive aspect of life.

- Be aware that the strongest influence which any adult can provide the child is the role model of his own positive attitudes and behaviors and attempt to behave accordingly.

- Rule out or discover and remediate any hormonal or other physical difficulty which may affect the outcome of your efforts. Then, be prepared to withstand the aggressive or passive behaviors of the child and to persevere for the length of time necessary to effect a positive, lasting change as the progress of our representative student, Roger, demonstrates.

Roger's parents have committed themselves to support him and his teacher in the behavior contract. Though they have experienced pain and sadness in implementing its negative consequences, they are heartened at the improvement they observe in his attitude and self-responsibility. His mother has not cleaned out his backpack nor sat at the table to monitor closely his homework production as in the past. Both have refrained from making comments about the lack of neatness of his papers and have only offered to quiz him because he misses several words on his spelling test each week. Neither of them has allowed Roger to be excused or explain away the fact that he neglected to initiate his contract or fulfill the desired behavior on certain days. They have celebrated his successes with the established simple rewards and have shown their pleasure and respect for his newly gained self-discipline by not undermining it with word or deed. During family discussions, they have shared more often and in detail their frustrations and fears when their own work projects and personal performances do not proceed as desired, as well as the feelings of elation they experience when they have persisted and achieved success. Both Roger and his parents have positive attitudes about his future.

Gifted Adolescent Females

Gifted learners appear in nearly every student population to some degree, and working with each type has its unique circumstances. Past research indicates that the adolescent female gifted student, for example, regresses in IQ significantly more than males, blocks her achievement when in competition with boys, and does not as often continue with math and science (Kerr, 1985). In addition, as adults, gifted women have not yet realized equity in salary, percentage of high-level jobs, or academic and economic level of achievement. Though there continues a trend for change in these areas, you may need to provide additional counseling and to suggest that training resources be implemented to empower your gifted girl students to develop their abilities more fully. Such resources would include defined strategies for facilitation of achievement and coping with success, mentor programs with established female professionals, and specialized career counseling. Training in assertiveness and effective use of power, as well as coping with anger, may also need to be considered. Such training will become increasingly unnecessary as parents and teachers consistently encourage girls and boys equally in areas across the curriculum and as women find equal opportunity in the workplace because of their different attitudes and training. Susan typifies the girl for whom these strategies may be warranted.

> **Susan** requires special consideration and advisement due to her extreme viewpoint and disposition. Her low tolerance for unfair situations as well as the drive to excel, represented by the compulsion to achieve all A and A+ grades on her elementary report card, have already placed undue stress upon her developing mind and body. She appears to suffer from body tension and could profit from learning relaxation exercises. Though her achievement is quite advanced, she does exhibit slightly less ability in mathematics and may require counseling to accept the fact that an A- or B+ in advanced mathematics classes may be a fine grade for her.

Culturally Diverse/Economically Disadvantaged

At the direction of the various departments of education, school districts increasingly have been admonished to provide appropriate education to high-potential children from under-represented diverse cultures or those who are economically disadvantaged. The difficulty in developing and implementing a successful identification process to discover these students has been discussed in the first chapter. Recent research has indicated that these children differ in their values as well as their preferred styles of learning. Their families and peers often are unsupportive of advanced education or present an inhibiting language barrier, and they are not always exposed to the enriched learning experiences necessary to their full development (Clark, 1988). It is exceptionally important for you to help discover these students early in their school careers so that the appropriate intervention can be implemented. Learning experiences must be provided, utilizing the

In addition, as adults, gifted women have not yet realized equity in salary, percentage of high-level jobs, or academic and economic level of achievement.

preferences of the groups of children involved, and needs to include experiences which may have been lacking in earlier years. Improvement in language skills is critical to their success. Your positive attitude and that of other teachers, among whom there should be a variety of cultures, toward working with this type of youngster is also important. Finally, your program must be flexible to accommodate these students' differences and should involve apprenticeships in higher-level work and academic counseling to break the existing pattern, as Maria's situation illustrates.

Maria exhibits to a minimal degree the characteristics germane to gifted girls coupled with cultural diversity when in my class. She clearly enjoys her social relationships and spends an equal amount of time with her friends and her studies. She continues in the honors mathematics track and her vocabulary increases slowly but consistently because of the high-quality discussions and literature she reads in her English honors classes. Her parents' native tongue is still the language of choice in their home, which provides her the bonus of being bilingual but does not enable them to promote correct English usage. There is no one who can help Maria edit her writing except her peers in read-around groups and her English teacher before school. She takes full advantage of the chances offered her for leadership responsibility and for advanced research studies in various areas. Her intermediate school counselor has already begun to discuss the many opportunities for advanced education and scholarships which can be hers if she maintains her present motivation and achievement.

Concluding Remarks

The challenge presented by struggling gifted youngsters is one which is vital for their supporters to meet. Many parents, teachers, and others in society feel antipathy toward education for the gifted because they are critical of these children who seem arbitrarily to refuse to fulfill the promise they possess. Moreover, as our society becomes increasingly complex and the family more convoluted, a higher percentage of bright children experience difficulty with achievement. Their academic futures, together with that of the mainstream of gifted children, rest largely in your hands as the teacher who creates, implements, and guides their learning experiences—the subject of the subsequent chapter.

> The challenge presented by struggling gifted youngsters is one which is vital for their supporters to meet.

What Does the Teacher of Gifted Students Need?

General Competencies

In any classroom, the most significant person is you, the teacher, who establishes and regulates the environment, enforces the discipline, sets the expectations, responds to your students' needs, and provides the myriad of other activities which are part of the learning experience. Purkey (1970, p. 43) states that the first task of a teacher is to "help each student gain a positive and realistic image of himself as a learner." To accomplish this end, the available evidence indicates that the teacher's attitudes toward herself and others is as important, if not more so, than her techniques, practices, or materials (Combs, 1969). Webb, Meckstroth, and Tolan (1982) agree that the way teachers behave, more than their knowledge, influences the degree to which students will learn. It is critical, therefore, for you to be a person who accepts, respects, and likes yourself so that you, in turn, can help to build the desired positive self-images and attitudes toward achievement in your students. The atmosphere you create must be one which is characterized by a great deal of challenge, a minimum of threat, and firm guidance. In addition, the beliefs conveyed about your students must be one

> The atmosphere you create must be one which is characterized by a great deal of challenge, a minimum of threat, and firm guidance.

of confidence in their success, with clear expectations and reasonable demands. Questions such as those listed below may be enlightening to you concerning your personal development in this area. You may want to jot down a number, 1–10, by each one to represent the degree to which you incorporate these attitudes into your teaching.

1	2	3	4	5	6	7	8	9	10
Not at All				Fairly Often					Very Often

- Do I encourage my students to take learning risks and to try new activities in and outside of school?
- Do I involve my students in planning classroom learning experiences and developing the class rules they follow?
- Do I minimize extreme competition in my classroom?
- Do I permit my students to question my thinking, and can I acknowledge my own areas of lesser strength?
- Do I share my honest feelings and treat my students in the positive, respectful way I like to be treated?
- Do I regularly schedule time when I can talk alone with each of my students?
- Do I make specific positive, as well as constructive, comments aloud, in notes, and on students' papers?
- Do I distribute my time fairly to each student, watching for times when certain ones may evidence a greater need?
- Do I perceive everyday disciplinary problems as unavoidable and not as personal insults?
- Do I have a clear idea of, and reinforce consistently, what is and is not acceptable in my classroom?
- Do I permit my students—and myself—the opportunity to make mistakes without penalty or a feeling of failure?
- Do I use a variety of learning experiences and teaching strategies over the year to guarantee success for all temperaments?
- Do I have high expectations for my own and my students' achievement and give specific praise for their progress?

It is also critical that you develop the awareness and intuition that enables you to assess the self-concepts of your students, allowing you to predict how they view themselves, others, and the world. The most effective strategy for accomplishing this task is through careful observation of their appearances and behaviors in different situations over time. Though you cannot climb into their skins,

Do I make specific positive, as well as constructive, comments aloud, in notes, and on students' papers?

you can train yourself to make relatively accurate assessments and recommendations for assistance in all but the most complex cases, as a review of Susan's and Bart's situations in my class exemplify.

> **Susan's** self-image is fragile because of her intensity and perfectionism. She is a steaming pressure cooker who, though she outperforms nearly everyone in my class, expresses a dissatisfaction with anything less than exceptional effort and achievement. Basking in the warmth of a well-earned accolade is nearly impossible for her because she must immediately direct her energies to the next demanding activity. I have counseled Susan and conferenced with her parents several times in an attempt to help her develop more equilibrium. I continue to use my need to accept less than perfection in my teaching as an example and have encouraged her parents to do the same type of modeling as relevant situations arise.

> **Bart,** on the other hand, already displays the balance and poise of a well-adjusted, though reticent, adult. I have encouraged him to accept leadership roles at many junctures, both to encourage his level of involvement and to allow other children to observe his emotionally and socially healthy role model. Even Susan is willing to work with Bart, and this has appeared to constitute my most successful intervention for her to this point.

The teacher in this environment would manage the classroom effectively, exhibit enthusiasm, initiative, resourcefulness, and creativity.

Specialty Training

Clark (1995, p. 1) describes the ideal learning environment and teacher to which every child should be entitled.

> *The classroom would be one that is attractive, organized, and conducive to learning. Such an environment would be rich in materials at many levels of learning, have simultaneous access to many activities that are varied and multisensory, and be flexible in grouping based on the needs of the learner. It would elicit students' responsibility, choice, trust, and cooperation. The teacher in this environment would manage the classroom effectively, exhibit enthusiasm, initiative, resourcefulness, and creativity. Teachers in every classroom need the ability to differ the pace of instruction, integrate the intellectual processes, assess the knowledge and understanding of the learner, and then present instruction so that each learner can benefit and progress to the highest level possible.*

31

Though this kind of high-quality instruction can result in success for all children, it exists so rarely that gifted students fail to fulfill their advanced potential in most classrooms where teachers with the wide spectrum of students inevitably choose to emphasize remedial needs. Designated groupings of gifted students, therefore, become necessary, taught by those who demonstrate an affinity for this type of student. The literature on gifted education contains many ideas about what professional qualities these teachers should possess.

> Designated groupings of gifted students, therefore, become necessary, taught by those who demonstrate an affinity for this type of student.

- ◆ Understand the characteristics of gifted students sufficiently to begin their identification process with accuracy and to represent individuals with specific case study data at the point of the final decision for placement.

- ◆ Understand the concept of learning styles, the way in which it influences gifted learners, as well as strategies to modify the learning environment and activities to fit the styles of individual students.

- ◆ Understand that gifted children have differing social/emotional needs that impact their learning and be able to apply appropriate strategies enabling them to progress to their highest level of maturity.

- ◆ Understand the curricular needs that result from the demands of giftedness and be able to apply the appropriate teaching strategies to vary the pace of the curriculum through acceleration and to differentiate the content, process, product, and/or learning environment.

- ◆ Understand how the home and school environments, as well as the personal qualities of gifted students, cause some to achieve at levels far below their potentials and be able to apply appropriate, long-term interventions.

- ◆ Understand that gifted students need the challenge of participation with their mental peers and employ strategies to meet that need by providing a variety of options in the learning environment.

- ◆ Understand and seek involvement as a team member to work with other teachers of the gifted and other staff to provide the best possible school services for gifted students.

Gallagher (1985) compares the difference between the regular classroom teacher and the teacher of the gifted to that existing between the general practitioner and the specialist in the medical field. Society easily accepts the concept that though the G.P. should have knowledge of basic surgery techniques, we would expect the heart surgeon to perform all by-pass surgeries. Just as this has no negative implication, neither should the skill and ability of the general educator be questioned because the teacher of gifted learners requires specialized education.

Personal Qualities and Knowledge

◆ Lists of the desirable personal characteristics of the teacher of gifted are so exaggerated in the literature that you may believe she must be larger than life. Those essential qualities, including the strong sense of self already discussed, are certainly attainable.

◆ A working knowledge of a variety of topics is needed in order to facilitate the interests of your students as well as to maintain their respect by interacting in a significant way.

◆ A high degree of energy and the ability to manage multiple activities is important to motivate the constantly active minds and bodies of your students.

◆ A well-developed sense of humor allows you to relate in a non-threatened manner to the sharp, quick wit of your students.

◆ The ability to lead when necessary and to facilitate whenever possible and appropriate enables you to encourage the growth of their leadership while maintaining an adequately controlled environment conducive to learning.

◆ An openness to change and the flexibility to alter the established schedule or lesson in favor of the "teachable moment" causes you to focus upon the quality of the learning process rather than the coverage of material.

◆ Genuine interest in and understanding of the gifted personality, including those qualities that can appear at first to be negative, enables you to avoid inappropriate and unnecessary confrontation.

◆ An acceptance of personal limitations, as well as an orientation toward self-growth and high level achievement in your areas of interest, creates a positive role model for your students.

Lists of the desirable personal characteristics of the teacher of gifted are so exaggerated in the literature that you may believe she must be larger than life.

33

◆ The ability to communicate effectively both orally and in writing facilitates this development in your students.

◆ A thorough understanding of and the ability to teach the processes of research—historical, experimental, and descriptive—are critical because gifted students need to be able to explore areas of interest and learning in a more complex manner much earlier than other students.

◆ The perspective which allows you to understand and elaborate upon the interrelatedness of ideas across the curriculum is necessary to facilitate your students' development of a fabric of integrated learning.

◆ The management and organizational ability to coordinate the involvement of parents of gifted learners in positive support of their children and the advocacy of their appropriate education is imperative as they are often as challenging as their children.

The ability to communicate effectively both orally and in writing facilitates this development in your students.

Specialty Preparation and Training

You may ask where it is possible to locate such individuals as are described above. The answer is that many suitable candidates are already teaching in our regular classrooms or are presently in teacher training. The qualities described above are partly a function of personality and teaching style and can be observed by administrators and other teachers already working with gifted learners, and those likely individuals can be encouraged to become involved. Obtaining the necessary preparation is easier than in the past, since nearly 140 colleges and universities in more than three-fourths of the states currently offer some type of program to educators wishing to specialize in teaching gifted learners, with over 100 also offering master's or doctoral degrees (Clark, 1995). Finally, necessary aspects can be self-taught by participating in the plentiful staff development opportunities provided by school districts and organizations supporting the gifted, as well as by studying some of the abundant supply of published resources.

Basic Resources to Own

Because the process of internalizing the above information and concepts is best accomplished over time, I recommend that a variety of books, such as those listed below, become a part of your professional library. In addition, state frameworks should be read and utilized as your general guide about the advanced requirements for which you should be responsible.

Classroom Questions by Norris Sanders (1966) is a practical guide to cognitive questioning based upon Bloom's Taxonomy, an invaluable tool to utilize in curriculum development and discussions.

Guiding the Gifted Child by Webb, Meckstroth, & Tolan (1982) is a pragmatic resource to support the emotional and social development of gifted children and positive relationships among them, their parents, and peers.

People Types and Tiger Stripes by Gordon Lawrence (1987) is an introductory book regarding learning styles, personality types, and their use in the classroom. This knowledge is valuable both as an aid in planning a variety of learning experiences and as a strategy to teach better understanding of self and relationships with others.

Curriculum Compacting by Reis, Burns, & Renzulli (1993) is a comprehensive guidebook for streamlining the regular curriculum to make time for enrichment and includes detailed plans for its implementation.

Moral Reasoning by Galbraith & Jones (1976) is a teaching handbook for implementing Kohlberg's theory of moral development in the classroom. This six-stage theory should be experienced by discussing real and simulated classroom dilemmas to help your students proceed to higher stages.

Creative Problem Solving: An Introduction by Treffinger & Isaksen (1992) is a simple guide for teaching the six stages of this process to students. They are guided through a prescribed series of steps to reach resolution regarding a problem, a strategy developed by Parnes (1967).

Underachievement Syndrome Causes and Concerns by Rimm (1986) is a practical prescription for dealing successfully with underachieving gifted children and their parents.

Cooperative Learning by Spencer Kagan (1987) is a book filled with many types of learning activities where students work in defined groups on structured tasks, seeking not only successful completion of learning but socialization strategies during the process.

Other Support Personnel

The need for understanding and support for your students and you from other classroom teachers, service personnel such as administrative, guidance, speech, learning resource, etc., and classified staff should also be recognized. In addition to counseling your students about their responsibility to cooperate, providing information to these others about the children's differences and the

> The need for understanding and support for your students and you from other classroom teachers, service personnel such as administrative, guidance, speech, learning resource, etc., and classified staff should also be recognized.

strategies that enable you to avoid confrontation and produce co-operation can help to foster positive relationships. Moreover, the gifted learner is often mistakenly not considered for special needs services, and it is up to you to become this child's advocate when it is necessary. Finally, sharing your creative ideas, classroom goals, frustrations, successes, and needs with professional peers can help you and your gifted students to be perceived realistically and positively.

Concluding Remarks

Being a teacher of gifted learners certainly provides an exciting, sometimes exhausting, teaching challenge and promotes a high level of personal and professional growth for the interested educator. At first blush, it may appear to be an insurmountable task to fulfill the expectations presented here. However, in the words of one of my fellow teachers who has chosen this specialty, "I feel like I've gone to teacher heaven." The chemistry which occurs among gifted learners when the match is made between them and their enthusiastic, trained teacher is a delight to experience and to observe. A further key enabling this reaction to occur is the qualitative learning experience in which the students and you must engage, the subject of the next chapter.

What Experiences
Should the Gifted Have?

Long-Range Goals

A significant school experience for the gifted child should result in the accomplishment of a number of worthy goals, very few of which can be adequately measured by current tests. They are not mentioned in Goals 2000, the Improving America's Schools Act (1994), and there is no set of textbooks for teachers to implement. These goals can be attained as the result of a series of appropriate learning activities experienced over time. When this is achieved by the end of his formal education, the gifted child should have developed the following:

These goals can be attained as the result of a series of appropriate learning activities experienced over time.

- ◆ a core of knowledge about the world
- ◆ basic skills and a fabric of integrated-subject learning
- ◆ ability to think at higher levels
- ◆ desire and ability to research a topic for a purpose
- ◆ ability to communicate capably in writing, verbally, and non-verbally

- desire and competence to behave as a responsible citizen
- ability to problem-solve, convergently and divergently
- qualities of the sophisticated reader and a love of reading
- ability to make qualitative judgments in the arts and sciences
- desire to realize high personal goals and aspirations
- independence, discipline, and self-responsibility for learning
- ability to relate positively to self and others
- skill to provide quality leadership or to support as a follower
- ability to relate to a mentor in an area of interest
- lifelong love of learning

Personal and administrative barriers must be overcome and the effective strategies and teaching models incorporated into the meaningful education of the gifted child.

Personal and administrative barriers must be overcome and the effective strategies and teaching models incorporated into the meaningful education of the gifted child.

Core Knowledge

As postulated in Goals 2000, there exists a body of information that all people should learn in order to be informed citizens of the world. For gifted persons, this fund of knowledge can be more extensive, including cultural and physical geography; the spectrum of governments, economics, and political institutions; the history of various disciplines; philosophical tenets; languages; and the elements of the performing arts, sciences, and mathematics. Because of their common strength in long- and short-term memory, nearly every gifted youngster can retain such information like a dry sponge soaks up water. Obtaining appropriate resources at achievable reading comprehension levels and enabling the student to access such materials have been the greatest challenges for teachers in the early grades. With the advent of computer technology, even these inhibitors have been largely overcome.

The basic skills involved in language arts, i.e., reading, writing, listening, and speaking, the eight strands of mathematics, and the skills attainment strands in the social sciences and sciences are necessary for all students to learn. The advanced child is capable of mastering these in a shorter period of time and with fewer repetitions than other children. In fact, it is my opinion that the primary reason that some gifted children do not readily learn them is that they are caused to practice far longer and forced to wait until later grades to encounter these introductory experiences, thereby losing their original interest. Modifying practice assignments in the skills areas, making the amount contingent upon attending to detail and correctness, and accelerating their exposure, can increase the gifted child's motivation and degree of success. Power struggles and gaps in skill learning can be largely avoided by the mainstream of gifted children by implementiing these simple strategies.

Moreover, the precocious youngster should experience many discussions and activities designed to cause these strands of information to be woven into a fabric of learning much earlier and more comprehensively than his counterpart. With his advanced abstract thought processing ability, he is capable of integrating knowledge across disciplines but does not automatically make these connections unless he is challenged and taught to do so. It is this broad conceptual learning which influences the quality of thought and interaction among humans far beyond their years of formal education.

It has also been acknowledged that all children should learn to think at every level but that the degree of time and emphasis must vary.

High Level Thought and Problem Solving

Discussing the acquisition of integrated learning is impossible without reviewing the higher-level thought processes it requires. Bloom (1956) created a complex *Taxonomy of Educational Objectives: Handbook I: Cognitive Domain* in which he outlined an inordinate number of specific thinking skills which could be taught. Simplified versions of his work explain the lower levels of knowledge and comprehension followed by the application, analysis, synthesis, and evaluation levels which make use of that which is known and understood. Processes exemplified by verbs and products exemplified by nouns have been presented to educators in many forms, from a wheel to the webbed configuration shown on the next page, in order to make this information useful in curriculum development. It has also been acknowledged that all children should learn to think at every level but that the degree of time and emphasis must vary. The nongifted child will require more involvement at the beginning levels while the gifted youngster moves beyond to the advanced levels more rapidly and often.

Taxonomy Web

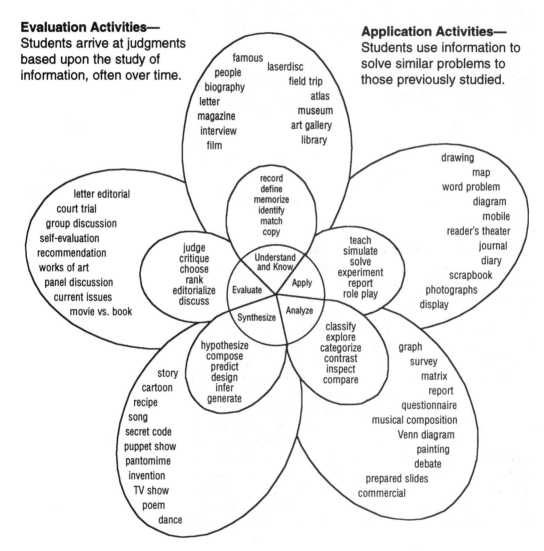

Knowledge/Comprehension Activities—Students learn and/or evidence an understanding of existing information.

Evaluation Activities—Students arrive at judgments based upon the study of information, often over time.

Application Activities—Students use information to solve similar problems to those previously studied.

famous
people
biography
letter
magazine
interview
film

laserdisc
field trip
atlas
museum
art gallery
library

drawing
map
word problem
diagram
mobile
reader's theater
journal
diary
scrapbook
photographs
display

letter editorial
court trial
group discussion
self-evaluation
recommendation
works of art
panel discussion
current issues
movie vs. book

record
define
memorize
identify
match
copy

judge
critique
choose
rank
editorialize
discuss

Understand
and Know

teach
simulate
solve
experiment
report
role play

Evaluate

Apply

Synthesize

Analyze

classify
explore
categorize
contrast
inspect
compare

graph
survey
matrix
report
questionnaire
musical composition
Venn diagram
painting
debate
prepared slides
commercial

story
cartoon
recipe
song
secret code
puppet show
pantomime
invention
TV show
poem
dance

hypothesize
compose
predict
design
infer
generate

Synthesis Activities—Students combine ideas or elements to make something different, new, or original.

Analysis Activities—Students examine the aspects, parts, or elements of ideas, identifying their relationship.

Solving problems using divergent (creative or synthesis level) and convergent (analysis level) thinking skills is a positive activity for all children but is essential to the bright child. A number of specific techniques have been developed which facilitate this type of thought processing. Brainstorming (Osborn, 1963) is a type of wild ideation where judgment is deferred until all novel ideas for solving a problem have been exhausted. Following this free-wheeling period, the ideas are evaluated, combined, or eliminated, based upon objective criteria. Attribute listing (Crawford, 1978) is a process during which all the various qualities of a problem or object are listed and changes or improvements recommended for each. The most promising of the suggestions can then be considered for implementation. In the morphological synthesis process (Allen, 1962), a matrix is created with the options for an aspect of a problem listed on one axis and those of another on the alternate axis. The two sets of options are forcibly combined in each cell of the matrix, and those judged most opportune are utilized. The synectics technique (Gordon, 1961) causes two seemingly unrelated ideas to be forced together with new perspectives becoming possible. You can utilize these well-defined strategies, and many others described in these authors' resources to enhance the gifted child's complexity of thought in the creative area.

Because language is the medium of the mind, it is imperative that each child learns to use it as effectively as possible.

Reader-Communicator

Because language is the medium of the mind, it is imperative that each child learns to use it as effectively as possible. The exchange of ideas through reading, listening, and the written and spoken word is the major exercise of the intellect, and the gifted child is capable of developing skill in this area. Once he has learned the basics of reading, the best way he can increase his skills, speed, and vocabulary is simply to read, read, and read some more. Too much emphasis upon phonics and stressing independent skills in isolation appears to hinder this progress, much as analyzing the gears of a bicycle might hinder the neophyte rider. The language arts program throughout his education should include as a mainstay the reading, discussion, and response to traditional and modern classics. These selections should be of the highest quality with regard to level of vocabulary, opportunity for interpretation, richness of description and character development, and universality of theme. Their authors should represent the best that has been written, said, or thought by man and should cross cultures and time. The gifted child should be caused to employ his high-level thought processing and problem-solving skills as he interacts with the characters and connects with such short stories, novels, poems, plays, and nonfiction as these brief examples from my curriculum illustrate.

Short Stories —"The Fog Horn" by Ray Bradbury, "The Big Wave" by Pearl S. Buck, "Lucky Boy" by Phillipa Pearce, "The Jumping Frog of Calaveras County" by Mark Twain

Novels—*The Talking Earth* by Jean Craighead George, *The Witch of Blackbird Pond* by Elizabeth George Speare, *Johnny Tremain* by Esther Forbes, *The Dark is Rising* sequence by Susan Cooper

Poems—"The Highwayman" by Alfred Noyes, "Paul Revere's Ride" by Henry Wadsworth Longfellow, "Sea Fever" by John Masefield, "Casey at the Bat" by Ernest Lawrence Thayer

Plays—"A Connecticut Yankee in King Arthur's Court" by Mark Twain, "Invasion from Mars" by H. G. Wells

Nonfiction—Essays: "The Mystery and Wonder of Words" by Maxwell Nurnberg, "Seeing" by Annie Dillard, "It All Started with Columbus" by Richard Armour, "The Crisis" by Thomas Paine, "What America Means to Me" by Jesse Stuart; Letters: "The Letters of Abigail Adams and John Adams," "A Letter from Thomas Jefferson to His Daughter;" Autobiography/Biography: "The Autobiography" by Benjamin Franklin, *George Washington's Breakfast* (and many other titles) by Jean Fritz

> By integrating some of the selections with themes and time periods in the social studies curriculum, the added feature of bringing the past to life can be accomplished.

Integration can be attained with relatively simple structures which cause the child to read widely and thoughtfully, write briefly but frequently, and listen and speak effectively as my Short Story Genre Assignment Sheet demonstrates. By integrating some of the selections with themes and time periods in the social studies curriculum, the added feature of bringing the past to life can be accomplished. That the genre focus upon real dilemmas faced by man and communicate his esthetic, ethical, and cultural values is inherently intriguing to gifted youngsters. This realization promotes the desire to read fine literature and write their own pieces for pleasure, rather than solely to fulfill class requirements.

Short Story Assignment Sheet

Name _____ Date _____

   I. Learn the twenty-one short story terms listed on the literary terms sheet for a quiz at the end of the unit.

  II. Read a minimum of ten, self-selected short stories chosen from the given short story authors list, including at least one of each type—adventure, mystery, science fiction, animal, fantasy, and human interest.

 III. Keep a short story record list of all those read, including the author, title, number of pages, and at least one of the terms on the literary forms list which you particularly noticed in the story.

 IV. Listen to, highlight vocabulary, reread, develop an interpretive question, and discuss the assigned three short stories.

  V. Complete a minimum of three story maps or plot lines for possible creative stories you might write.

 VI. Choose one of the story maps/plot lines and complete the writing process, including rough draft, read around, second rough draft, partner response sheet, third rough draft, parent response sheet, and final draft.

VII. Complete any optional extra credit activities chosen from the suggestions provided or developed by you.

VIII. Organize the above items into a booklet to be turned in for a final grade at the end of the unit.

Researcher–Independent, Disciplined Learner

The gifted learner possesses the curiosity and desire to discover what makes research a preferred activity. However, this raw talent, as with so many others germane to the gifted, must be harnessed and caused to work for him. As early as possible in his education, the precocious investigator should be taught the basic skills to locate, acquire, record, organize, and communicate information as the need for each arises during initial experiences. The effective and appropriate use of the wide variety of resources, both primary and secondary, the procedure to prepare information for a purpose, as well as the multiple means to present information to a variety of audiences, should be taught during increasingly sophisticated research projects. Selection of topics, types of sources, methods of presentation or product, and audiences can be afforded the child during independent study and provided by you with a degree of choice during in-depth curricular studies, as the partial list below demonstrates.

Projects assigned during each year must have as a continued goal the development of the discipline required for responsible, self-directed learning.

Topics—sign language, reptiles, pollution, robotics, dinosaurs, numismatics, sculpture, optics, colonial history, Indians, oceanography

Sources—books, media, interviews, museums, atlases, pamphlets

Product—radio show, filmstrip, demonstration, debate, diorama, report, game, poster, model, computer program, cartoon, poem, center

Audience—students, parents, school board, club, company, scientists

Pairing the gifted youngster with an adult mentor who shares and can facilitate learning can provide a most meaningful and memorable experience. Projects assigned during each year must have as a continued goal the development of the discipline required for responsible, self-directed learning. For example, throughout the fifth-grade year, each major integrated study for my class incorporates in-depth, organized research for a purpose.

- ◆ Preparation of an annotated American Indian picture book to read to primary students
- ◆ Construction and documentation of colonial technology for Weltesberg, an interactive museum
- ◆ Presentation of an American Revolutionary-period debate from a detailed prepared outline
- ◆ A formal, written research project on an inventor together with a creative, working invention

◆ A group-prepared audio-visual project regarding an aspect of the resolution of the slavery issue

◆ A group learning-center project which celebrates the diversity of cultures in America

Cultured Responsible Citizen

Each of the visual and performing arts expresses and embodies a significant portion of man's culture and should play a noteworthy part in the gifted child's curriculum. Rather than focusing solely upon the completion of crafts or holiday projects and productions, a study of the arts for these children should enable them to recognize, appreciate, and enjoy quality products in each field. High-caliber experiential activities, such as plays like "The Wizard of Oz," musicals like "Oliver," and studies of artists and styles like Van Gogh and impasto, shown on the following page, should certainly be undertaken. The children should be respected and treated in a professional manner as they perform their assigned roles or activities in these simulations. Both positions of leader and follower in group projects and simulations should be experienced repeatedly throughout their educations so that they are prepared to function effectively and meaningfully as adults.

In addition to the study of the sciences as subjects in the regular curriculum, gifted children should apply their high-level thought processing to some of their more debatable aspects such as environmental protection, genetic programming, and pollution. Learning early that there are issues where right depends at least in part upon a person's viewpoint and that opinion needs to be based upon a study of all sides is a most valuable and necessary lesson. Action taken through established procedures and channels to promote desired change completes the process. Long-term experiences such as these, together with the daily emphasis upon self-discipline and accountable independence within a classroom community, help to fulfill the goal of becoming a responsible adult citizen.

The children should be respected and treated in a professional manner as they perform their assigned roles or activities in these simulations.

Masterpiece: "Iris" *by Vincent van Gogh*

Concept:	Artistic Style
Grade:	Fifth
Lesson:	Impasto Painting

Objectives:

A. The students will explore a style of an artist.

B. The students will experience a new painting technique.

Vocabulary:

Impasto, Vincent van Gogh, Composition

Materials:

12" x 18" poster board
Tempera paint
White soap flakes
Water containers
Paint trays
Brushes

Process:

1. Draw a picture for your painting. It can be anything of your choice...be creative! Use good composition in arranging objects in your picture. Avoid using small details...they will not show up in the finished painting.

2. Impasto is a style of painting that Vincent van Gogh used. The paint is applied in a very thick, paste-like manner. The finished paintings will have a rough texture.

3. Mix about $\frac{1}{2}$ cup (125 ml) of soap flakes to one cup (250 ml) of tempera paint.

   * All paint varies for several reasons, so just mix until the right thickness; some paints will take more and some will take less soap. Mix until the paint is like a thick pancake batter.

Reprinted from TCM 018 Masterpiece of the Month, *Teacher Created Materials, 1990*

Positive Aspirer

Many a gifted child possesses a favorable view of himself and others, initially due to the positive responses he has received from his parents, extended family, and first friends. Whether this survives in the school setting is dependent upon the level of understanding of his teachers and the appropriateness of his curriculum and group experiences. If they are like the ones discussed above, his self-esteem will be strengthened and his positive relationships with others assured. In addition, his aspirations and goals will be commensurate with his high ability, and the gifted child will be well along the road to becoming a lifelong lover of learning.

Programs and Teaching Models

Each of these goal areas can be successfully incorporated as a part of the study of required subjects throughout the school years by teachers who have developed the necessary expertise. The gifted student should begin by being involved in a rigorous full-time elementary program which employs a variety of thought-provoking teaching models in a sequentially challenging curriculum. These should be followed by secondary enrichment and accelerated programs such as honors, humanities, and integrated studies courses and/or demanding comprehensive ones like the Advanced Placement (AP) and International Baccalaureate (IB). The former courses offer quantitatively greater information, as well as the integration of knowledge from related fields. The two latter programs involve the added dimension of formalized testing and, in the case of IB, several further specific requirements in order to obtain the full diploma. The AP exams are sponsored by the College Entrance Examination Board, and the four-year IB Program originates in Geneva, Switzerland. Both of these opportunities, when utilized fully, can gain the student a full year of credit at colleges and universities or, at the very least, excellent preparation for success at that level.

> Each of these goal areas can be successfully incorporated as a part of the study of required subjects throughout the school years by teachers who have developed the necessary expertise.

Taxonomies of Thinking, Feeling, and Morality

Teaching models which can challenge the minds of gifted children in a variety of subjects and domains abound in the educational literature. Those few presented here have been selected because they are relatively simple to understand and implement, yet they have proven to be very effective for me. Bloom's (1956) cognitive taxonomy governing intellectual development is accompanied by an affective taxonomy prepared by Krathwohl, Bloom, & Masia (1964). The general areas which indicate stages of development in the emotional domain are receiving, responding, valuing, organization of a value system, and demonstration of a personal philosophy of life. Activities and questioning can be

47

developed across the curricular areas to promote development of both the intellectual and emotional aspects of the mind. Kohlberg's (1969) moral development theory can also become influential in the gifted child's education through problem solving and discussion of moral dilemmas. The three sequentially higher levels include being obedient for selfish reasons like avoidance of punishment or gaining of rewards, conforming because of traditions such as majority rules or the dictates of the law, and concern for personal conscience and universal ethics.

Creative Problem-Solving Process

Though a number of models have been developed enabling students to experience the creative thought process, one which is quite practical to implement is that of Creative Problem Solving (CPS), outlined by Parnes (1967) and enhanced by Treffinger & Isaksen (1992). There are five stages: fact finding, problem finding, idea finding, solution finding, and acceptance finding. Each of these involves a divergent-thinking phase during which exhaustive lists of possibilities are developed, followed by a convergent-thinking phase during which the most likely options are pursued. Who, what, why, when, where, and how questions, encouraged at each stage, promote increased ideation. Using this process in the classroom to solve relevant and actual problems, like using the playground equipment equitably or gaining acceptance of a proposal to use land for an Indian cultural center, can help gifted children become habitual creative problem solvers.

The Simulation Process

The process of exploring a concept, issue, or dilemma by recreating an event in the classroom or school is called simulation. It may involve an hour, part or all of a day, or a number of hours over a several-week period, and can be designed or purchased for use in a number of subject areas. I conduct many personally prepared and commercially developed experiences each year, examples of which are included below.

◆ Turning into a greenhand for an overnight on the brig Pilgrim, made famous in R. H. Dana's novel, *Two Years Before the Mast*

◆ The Interact Company's "Dig II," "Galleons," "Pioneers," and "Invent" simulations

◆ Becoming an advertiser who completes and presents data gathered and analyzed in an officially conducted survey

◆ Teacher Created Materials' Geography Simulation experiences such as, Bus Stop, included on the next page.

> The process of exploring a concept, issue, or dilemma by recreating an event in the classroom or school is called simulation.

Bus Stop

Topic
Using map scale to find distance between locations

Objective
Students will use map scale to locate the geographic feature closest to a specific capital city.

Materials
- a continental map depicting both physical and political features of the area under study (one copy or textbook for each student)
- rulers with standard and metric measure for each student

Preparation
1. Copy, cut, and shuffle selected bus stop tickets. See the sample below.
2. Make copies of a continental map if a textbook is not being used.

Procedure
1. Divide students into heterogeneous cooperative learning teams of four members each.
2. Direct each team to choose a capital city in one of the countries in the continental region under study. No two teams should choose the same city.
3. Explain that the capital city they have chosen is to be their desired destination on a simulated bus tour. However, the bus may not go directly to their city. The object of the bus trip is to guess when the bus has come as close as it will get to their city. Be sure to tell students how many bus stops there will be on their trip so that teams can determine the odds of getting closer to their chosen capital.

Reprinted from TCM 483 Geography Simulations, *Teacher Created Materials, 1995*

Many gifted youngsters respond enthusiastically to this type of learning and willingly spend a great deal of time and effort in researching and preparing thoroughly to conduct the event in a realistic manner. The skills of cooperation, decision making, persuasion, and communication are necessary for successful simulating. Important benefits of this process are the development of a deeper level of understanding of people and events, attitudinal changes regarding debatable issues, and personal growth in leading and following. Debriefing in a thorough manner is recommended due to the students' intense involvement.

Cooperative Learning Model

To teach the skills necessary for effective group participation, a systematic model known as cooperative learning has been developed. Its stated purposes are to help students learn to solve group problems themselves, complete tasks and/or learn information, involve all group members in the work, and enjoy the process of working together (Dishon & O'Leary, 1984). This is an important activity for gifted children for several reasons. A percentage of bright youngsters resist becoming involved in any school groups, preferring to work and play alone. Their resistance can be due to past experience when the lion's share of the work was assumed by its most responsible members rather than spread equitably across the group. Another reason may be that the personality type and learning style of a particular gifted child make this process unappealing. Finally, the fact that many gifted youngsters like to dominate a group can bring about friction that they would rather avoid. In any case, humans do need to learn to recognize individual differences and to accomplish tasks that involve interacting with others. The formalized method of cooperative learning, with its established procedures and requirements, would seem to be a most positive and likely method to help the gifted student attain these skills. I use a number of cooperative learning techniques throughout my curriculum. For example, the jigsaw technique is one where each child is assigned to initial groups to read and learn about a specific aspect of early colonization. Students are then reorganized into new groups where each person is the teacher of his aspect, and the goal is for the new group to learn about all the topics. Designating roles, such as encourager, timer, retriever of materials, recorder, and spokesperson, to members of groups and debriefing about the skills learned along with the curriculum are effective cooperative learning techniques.

Enrichment Triad Model

Although there are any number of organizational models which have been developed to provide a framework for enrichment ac-

To teach the skills necessary for effective group participation, a systematic model known as cooperative learning has been developed.

50

tivities, Renzulli's (1977) Enrichment Triad Model is the best known and most often implemented. There are a number of practical, specific sourcebooks (Reis, Burns, & Renzulli, 1993) which can guide you in implementing the necessary strategies of curriculum compacting and investigative skills. As the word triad implies, there are three phases to this model; the first includes Type I enrichment which are general exploratory activities designed to expose the children to a wide variety of topics and areas of possible interest. The second phase, Type II enrichment, is that of group training activities designed to develop the intellectual and emotional/social skills necessary to investigation. The final phase, Type III enrichment, includes the examination and pursuit of real problems by individuals or small groups to accomplish a purpose.

Concluding Remarks

Due to their different learning styles and personality types, the students in your class will have particular favorites of the options described in this chapter. For example, my representative students, Roger and Susan, prefer independent study, he because of his atypical interests and she because it allows her to be in complete charge of her effort and achievement. Because of her need to control, she also has taken on many leadership roles as has Maria, who does so because she is conciliatory. Both girls, unlike Roger, who has difficulty in maintaining his focus in the freer atmosphere, enjoy simulation and the CPS process. Cooperative learning is a natural for Maria, while the introverted Susan and Roger are still reluctant in this activity. As might be expected, Bart seems to respond positively to all enrichment techniques, though he most often is in the background. The significant lesson to be learned from their reactions is that you must include a wide variety of experiences so that each student's personality type and learning style is valued, and everyone is provided the opportunity both to grow in areas of lesser inclination and to shine in preferred areas.

It is important for you to develop a working knowledge of the models and strategies presented above, as well as the internalization of the goals for your students' long-term education. Designing your own tailor-made curricular experiences and implementing them in the classroom can provide some of the greatest mental stimulation and satisfaction to you and the most relevant learning to your gifted students. However, when you understand the taxonomies and teaching methods presented in this book, you will also recognize those necessary ingredients in textbook questions and activities, not to mention those in other pub-

Due to their different learning styles and personality types, the students in your class will have particular favorites of the options described in this chapter.

lished resources on the market. Unlike thirty years ago, today you can find plenty of prepared programs, units of study, and activities which will excite and challenge your students with a reasonable degree of effort and organization on your part. A representative sample of these is the subject of the following chapter.

How Do I Create and Choose Their Curriculum?

Overview
At the center of any effective program for gifted youngsters should remain the principle of changing the pace, content, process, product, and/or environment to accommodate the more advanced levels they require. With the multitude of commercial materials, technology, and programs existing today, you can accomplish this with relative ease when you have sufficient understanding to choose and make suitable adaptations. The manner in which such materials can be implemented will depend upon the organizational structure of the gifted program in your school, i.e., pull-out with specialist, cluster within the regular class, or gifted/honors class, a topic explored later in this book. However, the ideas outlined below can be successfully implemented in any of these environments.

Change of Pace
Textbooks and many other school district materials, as well as requirements, have been developed with the gifted child as an afterthought. They can be made more appropriate for your advanced

Textbooks and many other school district materials, as well as requirements, have been developed with the gifted child as an afterthought.

students by acceleration or telescoping or by using the curriculum compacting technique mentioned previously as one aspect of the Enrichment Triad Model. Perhaps the simplest technique to implement is for you to condense or telescope the assignments for gifted children within your classroom curriculum. For example, while the rest of the class is studying selected stories from a unit in a literature-based reading text, you might assign the gifted child to read the entire unit and write an essay that judges the validity of the theme chosen by the publisher for that unit, citing evidence from each story. If a group of advanced youngsters completes the study, a discussion might augment or replace the written essay. In mathematics during a unit on fractions, your gifted child's assignment might include fewer practice problems, subject to their correctness, and extend his development by the creation of a fraction game to reinforce the other children's understanding. In science, with extra time gained from silently reading the assignment the class reads aloud, he might develop and gather materials to conduct a simple experiment which illustrates the concept being taught. Each of these alterations, involving only a flexible attitude and a few moments of planning time for you, can make a marked difference in the significance of your gifted student's school experience. He is rewarded for completing his work efficiently, is using important higher level skills, is developing independence, and is benefiting your class as a whole.

Curriculum compacting is a beneficial and more elaborate method of changing the pace and quality of your gifted student's school experience.

Acceleration of content is a technique most clearly exemplified in secondary programs like Julian Stanley's (1991) original Studies of Mathematically Precocious Youth (SMPY) at Johns Hopkins University. Each year across the United States, talented 6–12th grade math students are identified by SAT-M test scores and enrolled in summer or Saturday courses which further their knowledge far beyond their current grade level offerings. Most Talent Search programs now also discover youngsters who are verbally precocious, using SAT-V scores. The most notable searches are sponsored by Northwestern University, Duke University, University of Denver, and Johns Hopkins. Acceleration is also a major feature of such strategies as summer camps in specialty areas, concurrent enrollment at two school levels, and advanced placement courses, in addition to entirely specialized high schools. Finally, this technique is often used in elementary schools when students, especially in math, are given the opportunity to utilize the textbook beyond their grade levels and taught advanced skills not scheduled as competencies for their grades.

Curriculum compacting is a beneficial and more elaborate method of changing the pace and quality of your gifted student's school experience. It involves the pre and post testing of content in one or more areas to create time for enrichment while guaranteeing proficiency in the requirements. The evidence provided by the testing is of benefit to the child, who understands the need for the work he is asked to do, as well as to you and his parents who want to ensure that gaps are not created in his skill development. Representative books (Reis, Burns, & Renzulli, 1993; Renzulli, 1977) which provide step-by-step guidance are listed in the references. Enrichment activities to replace the work that has been compacted can include more complex, abstract ideas from the same subject area or might address independent or small-group work on a topic of your choice or theirs. Some representative ideas, followed by national sources for recognition, are listed below. Programs specific to your geographical area can be researched by the enterprising parent of one of your gifted students.

Programs specific to your geographical area can be researched by the enterprising parent of one of your gifted students.

◆ A Type III, Enrichment Triad project which addresses a real problem existing in the community

◆ Creation of a learning center or presentation to teach about a topic of interest with established requirements, including information with follow-up, an original game with board and pieces, a hands-on experience, audio-visual, or other items

◆ Preparation for an academic competition appropriate to the age and facilitated by the teacher, aide, or a trained parent

◆ A mentorship project where the child works with an adult sponsor over an extended period on a topic of common interest

◆ Independent study on a topic of interest with a preestablished contract to govern the process and presentation to an audience

◆ Scientific research culminating in a display, presentation, or entry into a local science fair

◆ Use of a computer program or other technology to consume further knowledge in a subject area or to produce a program or project for an audience

◆ Writing of original work(s) and publishing in an appropriate arena

Math/Science Contests

Mathcounts (Grades 7–8, teams) Mathcounts Foundation, 1420 King Street, Alexandria, VA 22314. School through national levels; increase prestige, awareness, improvement of mathematics

Mathematical Olympiads for Elementary Schools, Forest Road School, Valley Stream, NY 11582. School administered several times per year and sent in for scoring

ExploraVision Contest (Grades K–12, teams) Toshiba/NSTA ExploraVision Awards Program, 1840 Wilson Blvd., Arlington, VA 22201. Local through national levels; organized in various steps; involves development of future technology

International Science and Engineering Fairs, 1719 N Street, NW., Washington, D.C. 20036. Local through national levels; requires use of scientific method in experimentation

Humanities Contests and Publications

Adlyn M. Keffer Memorial Junior Short Story Writing Contest (Grades 4–12) National Story League, 561 Orchard Lane, Camp Hill, PA 17011. 2000 words or less of an original, correct story

Cobblestone Contests (Grades 5–9) Cobblestone Publishing, Inc., 30 Grove Street, Peterborough, NH 03458. Writing contests for readers of this American history magazine

Cricket League Contests (ages 5–9, 10–14) Carus Corporation, P.O. Box 300, Peru, IL 61354. Writing and art contests for readers of this magazine

Young Playwrights Project (Ages 12–18) John F. Kennedy Center for the Performing Arts, Very Special Arts Education Office, Washington, D.C. 20566. Encourages students to write about disability in contemporary society

National Geography Bee (Grades 4–8) National Geographic Society; 17th and M Streets, NW., Washington, D.C. 20036. Local through national levels; oral and written questions covering general knowledge of geography.

National History Day (Grades 6–12, individual or group) National History Day, 11201 Euclid Avenue, Cleveland, OH 44106. Local through national levels; seven categories, individual paper, individual or group projects, performances, or media

Reflections Program (K–12) National PTA Program Division, 700 N. Rush Street, Chicago, IL 60611-2571. Local through national levels; annual themes in four areas: literature, visual arts, photography, and music ideas

Young Writer's Contest (Grades 1–8) Young Writer's Foundation, P.O. Box 6092, McLean, VA 22106. National level; 500 words of less of any unpublished work written in current year

For additional information on contests in the humanities, write to:

> National Endowment for the Humanities
> Younger Scholars Guidelines, Room 316, Division of
> Fellowships and Seminars
> 1100 Pennsylvania Avenue, NW, Washington, D.C. 20506

General Areas/Creativity

Future Problem Solving Program (Grades K–3, 4–6, 7–9, 10–12, teams) Future Problem Solving Program, P.O. Box 98, 115 W. Main Street, Aberdeen, NC 28315. Local through international levels; year-long, organized, six-step process to solve scientific and social problems

Invent America! (Grades K–8) U.S. Patent Model Foundation, 510 King Street, Suite 420, Alexandria, VA 22314. Local through national levels; promotes creative thinking, scientific method, invention

Knowledge Master (Grades 7–9, teams) Academic Hallmark, P.O. Box 998, Durango, CO 81302. Computer administered biannually; tests of general knowledge in science, math, English, history, and trivia

Odyssey of the Mind Problem Solving (Grades K–5, 6–8, 9–12, teams) Odyssey of the Mind Association, Inc., P.O. Box 27, Glassboro, NJ 08028. Local through world levels; annual problems may include engineering, nonlinguistic, performance, etc.

U.S. Academic Decathlon Association (9–12) P.O. Box 5169, Cerritos, CA 90703-5169. Local through national levels; ten individual and team events; provides recognition and reward for academic endeavor

Additional Source of Information:

> Freed's Guide to Student Competitions and Publishing
> Judith M. Freed
> Department GT-400-M, 218 West Fountain Avenue
> Delaware, OH 43015

Content Change

When it is feasible and germane, the content in a subject or unit can be entirely different for gifted students. As part or all of their reading, the Junior Great Books program involving challenging stories, interpretive questioning, discussions and writing, might replace the regular basal reading series. Or a unit on geometric line designs, tessellations, and M. C. Escher might be implemented instead of the basic geometry unit included in the textbook. An

When it is feasible and germane, the content in a subject or unit can be entirely different for gifted students.

active simulation about the lives of the pioneers might replace the reading and follow-up questions of the social studies textbook chapter on the Westward Movement. Materials which make this type of substitution possible are plentiful and can be ordered from a variety of companies, some of which are listed below in alphabetical order. Though not an exhaustive list, these have been selected because they have been found to offer a large number of items which can be used effectively as presented or require the least amount of adaptation.

Activity Resources, P.O. Box 4875, Hayward, CA 94540
Materials designed to develop mathematical thinking of students through manipulatives, investigations, and games

Bright Ideas for Gifted and Talented, A.W. Peller & Associates, Inc., 210 Sixth Avenue, P.O. Box 106, Hawthorne, NJ 07507
Materials from 100 sources that are inquiry-oriented and emphasize problem solving and creativity

Creative Learning Press, P.O. Box 320, Mansfield Center, CT 06250
How-to, activity, interest-determining books for teachers and students, as well as computer software; publisher for Renzulli's books, as well as his followers

Creative Publications, 5623 W. 115th Street, Worth, IL 60482-9931
Materials from across the curriculum designed for hands-on experiences

Creatively Yours, Creative Education Foundation, 1050 Union Road, Buffalo, NY 14224
Source books for CPS, brainstorming, and leadership

Dale Seymour Publications, P.O. Box 10888, Palo Alto, CA 94303
Entire units for enriched study in math strands

Dandy Lion Publications, 3563 Sueldo, Suite L, San Luis Obispo, CA 93401
Units/source books from logic to research/independent study

DOK Publishers, 71 Radcliffe Road, Buffalo, NY 14214
Activities for students in the area of creative thought

Interact, 1825 Gillespie Way, #101, El Cajon, CA 92020-1095
Simulations in a variety of subject areas for elementary through high school grades

> Materials which make this type of substitution possible are plentiful and can be ordered from a variety of companies, some of which are listed below in alphabetical order.

Midwest Publications, P.O. Box 448, Pacific Grove, CA 93950-0448
Broad-based teaching of thinking skills through workbook exercises

Teacher Created Materials, Inc., P.O. Box 1040, Huntington Beach, CA 92647
Teacher-friendly source books and units from across the curriculum written by teachers for teachers

Thinking CAPS, Inc., P.O. Box 26239, Phoenix, AZ 85068
Task cards, porta-centers, and games on many topics

Zephyr Press, 3316 Chapel Avenue, P.O. Box 66006-B, Tucson, AZ 85728-6006
Materials to help students reach their highest potential, publisher of Gardner's Seven Intelligences and followers' materials

Process Change

The most necessary adaptation when using commercial materials with gifted children is to change the process, i.e., extend or alter the given idea to increase its complexity. Often, simply reviewing the suggestions and choosing the one or two most challenging ideas are all that is necessary. For these students, it is preferable to seek greater depth of thought concerning fewer topics. Moreover, a higher level question necessitates thought at that level and all others lower on the taxonomy. For example, in the literature replacement unit page "Extra! Extra! Extension Ideas," included on page 61 from *The Cricket in Times Square* (Onion, 1993) unit, a number of extension activities have been listed. Though each has some appeal, the direction to compare and contrast the film and the book, or to compare and contrast Tucker with Templeton mouse from *Charlotte's Web* (White, 1952), is at the level of analysis on Bloom's Taxonomy. To complete either of these activities, the reader must have knowledge of the story, comprehend the information about the characters and plot, and apply them to the given situation in order to complete the analytical thought process. Extending the activity to include the question, "Which medium did you prefer and why?" or "Which author created the more appealing character and why?" causes the student to jump to Bloom's highest level of thinking—evaluation—which includes all the prior levels, including synthesis.

On the other hand, some assignments may not necessitate any change in the prepared materials. For instance, A Journey Circle, included on page 62 from another literature unit, *A Christmas Carol* (Deleo-Augustine, 1993), appropriately directs individuals

> Often, simply reviewing the suggestions and choosing the one or two most challenging ideas are all that is necessary.

to analyze the effect on Scrooge of the various places he visited with Spirit of Christmas past, as well as to create an illustration of each place, a synthesis level activity.

A third technique of extending, or piggybacking, on a given idea is often possible. The activity Any Questions, shown on page 63, from *Roll of Thunder, Hear My Cry* (Levin, 1994), for example, asks students to develop answers to given questions the reader might have when the story closes. Using their creative or synthetic thinking to imagine what might have happened to various characters is already a higher level activity. However, a natural extension, adding even greater complexity and more appeal for gifted youngsters, might be to select one aspect and write an additional chapter which provides closure. Again, the activity Word Webs and the Greeks, on page 64, taken from *Ancient Greece* thematic unit (Jeffries, 1993), emphasizes vocabulary development through applying Greek word roots to related words in English. To extend this activity to the synthesis level, the assignment might be to create new words not yet invented. This could be accomplished by combining various Greek roots with known prefixes and suffixes and drawing a picture of what each depicts or by developing a definition.

A third technique of extending, or piggybacking, on a given idea is often possible.

Extra! Extra! Extension Ideas!

The following activities can be integrated into your unit as extensions to the activities already outlined in this book. Some of them may require a little more footwork or planning before presenting them to your class. The ideas are in no particular sequence or order.

- Make traditional ice cream sodas.
- Share a copy of the *New York Times* with your class. Create your own classroom newspaper modeled after it.
- Look at a Chinese restaurant's menu. Design your own Chinese menus.
- Have a Chinese person come to speak to your class about his/her culture.
- Bring in tapes of old radio show programming to play for your students.
- Plan a scavenger hunt to "scrounge" for objects like Tucker mouse.

- Keep a cricket in the classroom for students to study. Vote on a name for your new class pet.
- Play classical string ensemble and country "fiddle" music for your students. Compare the two styles of music and methods of playing the violin.
- Have a student or musician who plays a stringed instrument speak to and play for your class.
- Read some of George Selden's sequels (*Tucker's Countryside, Chester Cricket's New Home, Chester Cricket's Pigeon Ride*).
- Read *Charlotte's Web* by E.B. White. Compare and contrast Tucker and Templeton mouse.
- Watch the film of *A Cricket in Times Square*. Compare and contrast the novel and the film version.
- Take a field trip to your local newspaper, ride on a train or subway, or attend a classical string concert.

Reprinted from TCM 419 A Cricket in Times Square Literature Unit, *Teacher Created Materials, 1993*

A Journey Circle

Where did Scrooge go? What did he see?

Activity:

1. Dickens writes this section of the book as a flashback. Explain flashback (as an author's tool) to the students and examine why it is important to the story for Scrooge to relive his past.
2. Review with the students the places Spirit of Christmas past shows Scrooge—his boarding school, apprentice shop, the last meeting with his former girlfriend, and his former girlfriend's home.
3. Explain that each location has a significance to the spirit's lesson and a profound effect on Scrooge.
4. Duplicate the Journey Circle below for students to use.
5. Students will complete the Journey Circle by writing and illustrating the places Scrooge and the Spirit visit and explaining the effect each place has on Scrooge. (**Note to the teacher:** This worksheet could be completed by individual students as a quiz or by small groups as a way to help one another clarify the author's message.)

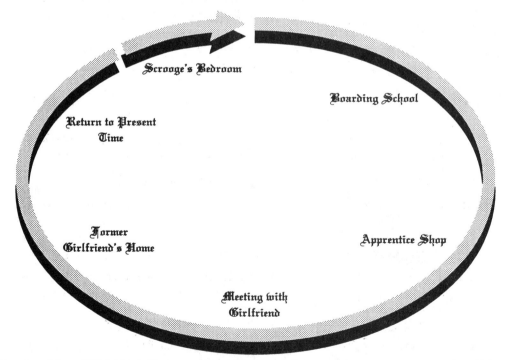

Reprinted from TCM 434 A Christmas Carol Literature Unit, *Teacher Created Materials, 1993*

Any Questions?

When you finished reading *Roll of Thunder, Hear My Cry*, did you have some questions that were left unanswered? Write them here.

_____

_____

_____

Now work in groups or by yourself to prepare possible answers for the questions you asked above or those printed below. When you finish, share your ideas with the class.

- Did Mama ever get her teaching job back?
- What happens to T.J.?
- Are R.W. and Melvin Simms ever charged with the murder of Mr. Barnett?
- Does Papa go back to work on the railroad?
- Does Mr. Morrison stay with the family?
- Are the Logans able to keep their land? If so, how?
- Is Jeremy ever accepted as a friend by the Logan family?
- Does the family ever discuss how the fire began?
- Is the Logan family able to send Cassie away to high school or college?
- What is Uncle Hammer's occupation?
- Is there ever peace between the whites and blacks so the Logan family does not have to live in fear?
- Do the black children and white children ever go to the same school?
- Will Cassie ever be able to control her temper?
- Do Lillian Jean and Cassie ever speak again?
- Does Mr. Jamison remain friends with the Logans?
- After Mama is fired, who takes her place? Describe Stacey's new teacher.

Word Webs and the Greeks

Etymology is the study of words and their origins. Many words we know originally came from the Greek language, and they were first used by the Greeks of the periods you are studying.

Pysche is one such word. It is the Greek word for "soul." It exists in many forms in our language. Look at the word wheel below.

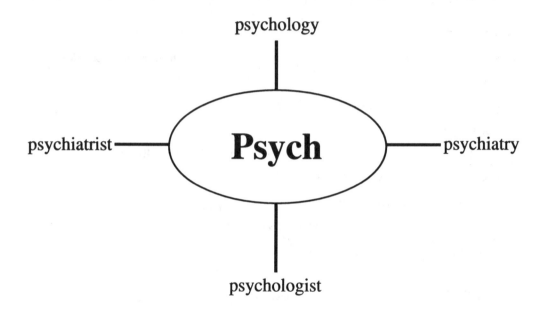

Here are three more Greek words: *ecos* meaning house, *demos* meaning people, and *polis* meaning city. Fill in the wheel for each word. Add spokes as needed.

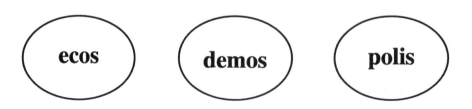

Reprinted from TCM 297 Ancient Greece Thematic Unit, *Teacher Created Materials, 1993*

Location or Personnel Change

Changing the environment in which your gifted students learn is a final method for appropriately differentiating their educational experience. Field trips to other places of learning can bring to life studies that originate in your classroom. Whether as an individual or in groups, gifted youngsters benefit from the opportunity to view items firsthand and to ask questions or discuss issues with expert docents. On the other hand, simply moving to a different part of the school, such as the library, multipurpose room, or to the outdoors, for your learning can help to motivate these children's desire to produce exciting ideas. Opportunities for guest speakers who can enrich a topic of study with a detailed presentation should also be provided. Quite often, merely the visitation of performers to the class of gifted children following a school-wide show can be a meaningful behind-the-scenes experience for both parties. Not to be overlooked are the human resources that parents of your gifted youngsters can be or the visitations or presentations they can arrange.

My representative students demonstrate how the above accommodations affect their educational experience in our classroom.

Changing the environment in which your gifted students learn is a final method for appropriately differentiating their educational experience.

> **Susan, Bart, Maria,** and **Roger** are immersed in the classroom curriculum to different degrees and in different ways. Susan's and Bart's assignments in the basic skills of language and mathematics have been compacted, and they have contracted with me to research independently about the deterioration of the rain forest. Both students are excited to present the data collected and their recommendations to the local office of the Environmental Protection Agency in the form of a videotape. I have shared my file of resources, including books and teaching units that provide some initial background information and ideas. The pair has made arrangements with their parents to be transported to the nearby university library to conduct more sophisticated research to discover individuals they might interview and other influential groups to whom they might present their product. I have promised to take them to the district video production room at the appropriate time so that they can edit their several hours of videotaped work. Roger continues to progress in his efforts to organize his time, materials, and work to accomplish the required work in my class. During the weekly period when all the students in my class may contract for an independent study of their choice, he has become involved in designing a computerized version of his cartoon characters. I have given him several district materi-

als ordered with him in mind, as well as names and addresses of cartoonists and their publishers, and he intends to forward his work for their review. He is motivated, for the first time, to learn the correct format and skills necessary to write business letters which will impress these adults and is working individually on these at the computer, using one of my CDs on this topic. Maria continues with the regular honors English reading at the junior high level but has become immersed in a special audiotaped vocabulary program designed to prepare students for success on the SAT test. In addition, her math teacher has telescoped her practice work in each of his units, and she is involved in the creation of creative support materials for math. They are written in her second language to enable other students who share her culture difference to succeed in learning the concepts, and she is excited about mathematics for the first time.

Concluding Remarks

Though it is helpful to examine each of the elements of differentiation individually for the purposes of discussion, very often you will incorporate several or all into an enriched experience for gifted children.

When the appropriate combination is provided, whether it is from teacher-developed or commercial materials or established programs, your students will become stimulated to reach the higher levels of thought, discussion, and questioning that are necessary to the full development of their potential. The challenge is not to locate a sufficient quantity of prepared materials but to make discerning choices which employ only those of the highest quality. Often, the early experiences provided to a gifted youngster are piecemeal, unrelated, and extraneous rather than interwoven into a consequential fabric of integrated learning. Counteracting this trend in his education must be his parents who should work in support of each teacher and their child. This is the final key to his desirable education and the subject of the next chapter.

Often, the early experiences provided to a gifted youngster are piecemeal, unrelated, and extraneous rather than interwoven into a consequential fabric of integrated learning.

What Should Parents of the Gifted Do?

Questions, Questions

All mothers and fathers face similar challenges in raising their children successfully, and the parent of a gifted youngster is no exception. However, the gifted offspring does present additional considerations. Is he really all that different? Should his ability be denied so that he can be "normal" or emphasized so that he maximizes his potential? Shouldn't he be outstanding in all subject areas because of his ability? Should I be closely involved in his schoolwork or make it his total responsibility? Should I carefully monitor his education, or will his teachers think I am a pushy parent? What kind of school program is best for him? Should he be involved in each of the activities in which he expresses an interest or talent, or will he experience burn out? Each of these questions is real to you as parents of a gifted child and must be resolved in order for his education to be successful.

Nature v. Nurture

When a child is found to be gifted, there is evidence that you have already accomplished much that is positive—both in terms of

All mothers and fathers face similar challenges in raising their children successfully, and the parent of a gifted youngster is no exception.

67

nature and nurture—before your child entered school and, most often, have done so with little formal guidance. How much of the success can be contributed to your genetic heritage and what percentage is due to the environment you have provided has been the subject of much debate over the years. In fact, research indicates that all brain processes necessary for giftedness are present at birth in almost every human but will deteriorate if the stimulation needed to activate them is not generated. When the enriched environment that speeds up the brain cells' activity and strengthens them is provided, the child experiences an advancement at the cellular level, becomes increasingly biologically different, and, with sufficient consistency, functions at a gifted level. Genes provide programs for individual potential, but the physical conditions beginning at the embryo stage may alter the direction and degree of development (Clark, 1988). Whatever the ratio, Guilford (1967) clarified the nature v. nurture issue by postulating that each establishes a ceiling on intellectual development and that individuals rarely achieve to the upper limit of either their hereditary or environmental possibilities.

Most often the gifted child showed an unusual alertness and interest in the world, as well as a concern for its welfare.

Degree of Difference

Though they may not, at the time, have been aware of distinctive differences, many parents of gifted children, when asked to reflect, have reported a number of qualities noted early. Most often the gifted child showed an unusual alertness and interest in the world, as well as a concern for its welfare. He commonly exhibited early development of complex vocabulary and abstract language and read at an early age. A remarkable storage and memory for facts, as well as a persistent curiosity and questioning about the way things work, are added factors reported by parents. Finally, a great degree of energy and genuine friendships with older children and adults also was noticed by parents. These qualities are not exhibited to the same intensity by the spectrum of children and do make obvious the gifted child's differences. Moreover, if one accepts that at least one of the intelligences can be partially defined by the administration and analysis of an individual IQ test, then the normal curve, with its corresponding percentiles, standard deviations, and intelligence classifications, demonstrates the differences that exist among gifted, average, and mentally deficient persons.

As mentioned in Chapter 1, a child is generally called gifted if he scores 130 (98th percentile/very superior range) or above on an individual IQ test. This score is as far from that of 100 (50th percentile/average range) as the child who scores 70 or below (mentally deficient range). It is not difficult for the parents of a child with an IQ of 70 or below to understand that he has special needs and demand that he be provided a unique program of education to maximize his potential; the same realization should exist for you as the parents of a child who scores 130 or above. The gifted youngster who may be skilled at masking his ability—or may not be fully aware of it—requires a challenging educational program in order to develop, rather than to dissipate, his capabilities. Furthermore, this youngster's primary advocates must be you who should resist the idea that you need to apologize for or downplay those unique needs which must be addressed. On the other hand, it is unwise to encourage the child to develop a false sense of importance because of his scores on an IQ test. It is also essential for you to maintain a reasonable stance with the adults responsible for your child's learning, not appearing to satisfy your own ego needs through this youngster. However, you cannot abandon your responsibility to persist in asking thoughtful questions about your gifted child's program until you receive sensible answers and see positive results. When your child attends his class with a sense of anticipation and you can observe that the work requires a substantial degree of effort and results in his positive satisfaction, you can relax your vigil.

> In our society, labels are an established fact and in fields such as sports seem to cause no complaint.

To Label or Not

In our society, labels are an established fact and in fields such as sports seem to cause no complaint. Moreover, labels have become a requirement for entrance into special education programs, primarily because money has been earmarked for the support of those so designated. In order that these funds not be used for other purposes, stringent regulations have been developed that must be documented for any student who is to be included. In any case, a gifted child recognizes from an early age that he is different with or without a label; whether this is perceived as a positive or negative difference is largely determined by the reactions of his parents, teachers, and peers.

The label can cause a problem, depending on the way in which it is explained initially and validated later. If your child is helped to understand that he is similar to others in many respects but is also different in certain abilities, he is likely to perceive himself as a unique, but not better, human being. If being gifted is explained simply as signifying the point in his development where he needs to learn at a faster pace and with more thought to remain excited about school and learning, he is unlikely to determine that he is superior to another child who does not yet exhibit that need. Should he be grouped with other children who share many of his differentiated needs, he is unlikely to perceive himself as brighter in all areas than the other students around him. If he is involved in challenging activities which require his full effort, he is unlikely to learn that he can earn A's with little or no exertion. Should he be empowered to respond with indifference to other children who react negatively to the label or to some of his unusual qualities, he is unlikely to be singled out for continued harassment. If he is guided to develop into a reasonably well-rounded individual with realistic expectations of himself and others, he is likely to be seen as a positive, popular leader. Providing this kind of guidance may seem like an awesome task to you as the parents of a gifted child; though it certainly represents a significant challenge, maintaining a moderate, reasonable attitude is the most important factor to ensure success.

Overall or Specific Ability

A gifted child may have fairly evenly developed unusual abilities, or he may be advanced in one or two areas and relatively average in others.

A gifted child may have fairly evenly developed unusual abilities, or he may be advanced in one or two areas and relatively average in others. When a Wechsler IQ test has been administered, the review of his subtest scores, detailed in Chapter 1, can reveal to some degree which tendency exists. While the youngster with a consistent pattern generally can be expected to function relatively well in school, the one with prominent peaks and valleys in his profile is likely to exhibit frustration. This can perhaps be explained because many gifted youngsters manifest tendencies toward perfectionism. Those who are consistently unable to realize the vision of their performance in one or more areas can develop self-doubts like the young girl I heard lament, "Why can't I figure out math and read quickly like I can write poetry?" The evenly developed perfectionist also can experience difficulty in determining when he has done his best work. For this child, the vision of what could be possible encounters time and energy constraints, causing the child to express dissatisfaction even with a product which his parents and teachers perceive as remarkable. Modifying this situation is difficult and involves time, patience, and modeling of the behavioral process which exhibits compromise and reasonableness.

How Much Is Too Much?

A certain degree of stress is healthy for humans to function satisfactorily as defined by the Yerkes-Dodson law. However, beyond the point of maximum efficiency, which varies among people and types of tasks, added stress begins to cause a decrease in adequacy, leading to extreme disorganization at its peak (Hebb, 1972). Since you are the most significant other to your child, you must be careful to give clear and consistent positive messages to your child regarding his self-expectations, along with constructive criticism which you may believe is necessary. Double messages or those that indicate your need to enhance your child's work should be avoided (Davis & Rimm, 1985).

It is critical to your gifted child's development that he be allowed to make mistakes without experiencing the stress of being judged or judging himself to be a failure. He needs to feel empowered to deal with his environment and supported when he falls and skins his emotional, social, or intellectual knees. These situations should be seen as setbacks along a continuum of success and as evidence of his willingness to take healthy risks. Using stories like that of Thomas Edison's infinite enthusiasm and patience during his many failures to develop a light bulb can be meaningful. Children are amazed to discover that he performed several thousand experiments using different filaments before he found one that finally enabled him to succeed.

You need to help your child evaluate what is the worst-case scenario for a failure, including experiences in figuring overall grade averages when a poor grade in a subject has occurred. Simply practicing active listening where you paraphrase back to your child what he has said and validate his feelings can provide the necessary support for him to deal successfully with that experience. Identifying the problem and establishing strategies for rectifying future similar situations are important to accomplish when he is ready. The questions "How will you do this differently next time?" and "What did you learn from this situation that you can use in the future?" can be of the greatest value. In addition, this perceptive person will need to become involved at an appropriate juncture in evaluating his areas of greater and lesser strength so that realistic expectations can be established for what constitutes success in each. Finally, relief can be the result of the child accepting the fact that he cannot always win and that one failing experience does not make him a failure. Channeling your gifted youngster into some noncompetitive activities such as hobbies, research, and family field trips can balance those in which he may feel intense pressure.

Often, your child has the ability to become accomplished in almost every area he encounters, which can be a pressure in itself. Initially, it is appropriate for him to experiment with various activities to determine his most intense interests. However, as school, studies, social life, and outside enrichment become increasingly demanding, choices from among them become necessary so that your child does not find himself in a disorganized state of frustration. Helping him to prioritize his activities, sharp-

It is critical to your gifted child's development that he be allowed to make mistakes without experiencing the stress of being judged or judging himself to be a failure.

en his time management and organizational skills, and then make the difficult choices to eliminate the lower priorities can be an important service you provide. You can be a very effective one-to-one teacher but should be careful not to convey the impression to your child that he cannot achieve success without your involvement. You may also need to assist your child by giving valuable feedback to the teacher if he consistently is not responding to the challenges given in his schoolwork. Whatever your gifted child's level of involvement, it is critical that he accepts the idea that achieving his personal best in any situation should be the end goal of his job, which is being a school student, rather than winning every competition or succeeding readily in each experience.

School Involvement and Support

A number of possibilities exist for parents of gifted children to provide school support for their child. Your most important one is the consistent role of the encourager and "go-fer" who takes him places and helps to locate or obtain the resources and materials that help your child accomplish many of the ideas his mind can envision. One-to-one teaching or reinforcement of basic skills, facilitation of mastery of word processing skills, and help in editing his writing are often necessary tasks for you. Teaching tolerance, respect, and patience with siblings and schoolmates is also an issue for parents of children with certain personality types. Asking questions rather than lecturing, providing significant opportunities with guidance, and encouraging rather than pressuring will increase the likelihood that the channels of communication can remain open between you and your gifted child.

> At the elementary level, nearly every child feels a sense of happiness and security when one of his parents is able to work in his classroom.

At the elementary level, nearly every child feels a sense of happiness and security when one of his parents is able to work in his classroom. Doing so provides the added value of enabling you to become knowledgeable about the teacher's expectations and the class structure. Moreover, there is the distinct advantage that another pair of hands provides toward the amount of work that can be accomplished with these active and challenging students. Teachers of gifted students who are providing appropriate challenges for them, whether they teach an entire class or a cluster within a regular class, work extremely diligently and appreciate the active assistance provided by capable people.

By the secondary level, parents of gifted youngsters are most often involved in booster groups or other outside support activities. The adolescent gifted child may need another type of support and guidance without which his grades can drop because learning suddenly isn't "cool." Gifted girls may fear that they seem unfeminine or unattractive by succeeding in school and hide their knowledge and ability. You need to value and support your youngster during this period, not add to the difficulty by stressing social success.

You may find participation in discussion groups or attendance at conferences for the gifted to be a valuable means of support for yourself. Sharing stories of success or frustration, as well as learning strategies for dealing more effectively with your child, can make the difference between self-doubt and self-confidence. Often discussion opportunities or presentations are offered by local school districts and many county, state, and national conferences occur on an annual basis.

One final, but extremely important, function you as the parent of a gifted child would be wise to perform is that of the advocate for gifted programs and services. Small but active and dynamic groups of parents have many times saved the day during a critical juncture at the district, state, or national level. Listed below are several national advocacy groups which provide leadership in these endeavors. Your state may also have formed a group.

> You may find participation in discussion groups or attendance at conferences for the gifted to be a valuable means of support for yourself.

◆ Association for the Education of
Gifted Underachieving Students (A.E.G.U.S.)
P.O. Box 359
Bedford Hills, NY 10501

◆ Association for the Gifted
Council for Exceptional Children
1920 Association Drive
Reston, VA 22091

◆ National Association for Gifted Children
1155 15th Street N.W., Suite 1002
Washington, D.C. 20005

Concluding Remarks

With the current reform movement in Congress, Newt Gingrich (1995) has made this statement which could be a harbinger of good fortune for the bright youth of our country. "If young people were to learn from school and the media that the future could be better—if more teachers were to become infected with the idea that the twenty-first century will be a century of opportunity—there would be a remarkably different mood in America....The challenge for us is to...put scientists, engineers, entrepreneurs, and adventurers back into the business of exploration and discovery."

References

Adderholdt-Elliot, M. (1987). Perfectionism. Minneapolis, MN: Free Spirit.

Allen, M. S. (1962). Morphological creativity. Englewood Cliffs, NJ: Prentice-Hall.

Alvino, J. (1989). Psychological type: Implications for gifted. Gifted Children's Monthly 10(4), 1–3, 23.

America 2000: An education strategy. (1991). Washington, DC: U.S. Department of Education.

Bloom, B. (1956). Taxonomy of educational objectives. Handbook I: Cognitive domain. New York: David McKay.

Carroll, H. A. (1940). Genius in the making. New York: McGraw-Hill.

Clark, B. (1988). Growing up gifted (3rd ed.) Columbus, OH: Merrill.

Clark, B. (1995). Teaching gifted learners: A specialized area of professional development. The Journal of the California Association for the Gifted 26(3), 1, 32–33.

Combs, A. W. (1969). Florida studies in the helping professions. (Social Science Monograph, No. 37). Gainesville, FL: University of Florida Press.

Cox, J., Daniel, N., & Boston, B. O. (1985). Educating able learners, programs and promising practices. Austin, TX: University of Texas Press.

Crawford, R. P. (1978). The techniques of creative thinking: Training creative thinking. Melbourne, FL: Krieger.

Davis, G. A., & Rimm, S. B. (1985). Education of the gifted and talented. Englewood Cliffs, NJ: Prentice-Hall, Inc.

Deleo-Augustine, J. (1993). A Christmas carol. Westminster, CA: Teacher Created Materials.

Dishon, D., & O'Leary, P. W. (1984). A guidebook for cooperative learning: A technique for creating more effective schools. Holmes Beach, FL: Learning Publications.

Education Consolidation and Improvement Act. (1981). Public Law 97-35.

Galbraith, R. E., & Jones, T. M. (1976). Moral reasoning: A teaching handbook for adapting Kohlberg to the classroom. St. Paul, MN: Greenhaven Press, Inc.

Gallagher, J. (1985). welcome datacomp. Boston, MA: Allyn and Bacon.

Gardner, H. (1983). Frames of mind: The theory of multiple intelligences. New York: Basic Books.

Gingrich, N. (1995). To renew America. New York: Harper Collins Publishers.

Goals 2000, safer schools, family involvement, individual education accounts, school-to-work, improving America's Schools Act. (1994). Washington, DC: U.S. Department of Education. Gordon, W. J. (1961). Synectics. New York: Harper & Row.

Guilford, J. P. (1967). The nature of human intelligence. New York: McGraw-Hill.

Hebb, D.O. (1972). Textbook of psychology. Philadelphia, PA: W.B. Saunders.

Hildreth, G. (1952). Educating gifted children at Hunter College Elementary School. New York: Harper and Brothers.

Hildreth, G. (1966). Introduction to the gifted. New York: McGraw-Hill.

Jeffries, D. (1993). Ancient Greece. Westminster, CA: Teacher Created Materials.

Jung, C. (1933). Psychological types. New York: Harcourt.

Kagan, S. (1988). Cooperative learning. Laguna Niguel, CA: Resources for Teachers.

Karnes, M. B. (1986). <u>The underserved: Our young gifted children</u>. Reston, VA: Coucil for Exceptional Children.

Kerr, B. A. (1985). <u>Smart girls, gifted women</u>. Columbus, OH: Ohio Psychology Publishing.

Kohlberg, L. (1969). <u>The cognitive-developmental approach to moral education. Moral education...it comes with the territory</u>. Berkeley, CA: McCutchan Publishing.

Krathwohl, D., Bloom, B., & Masia, B. (1964) <u>Taxonomy of educational objectives. Handbook II: Affective domain</u>. New York: David McKay.

Lawrence, G. (1987). <u>People types and tiger stripes: A practical guide to learning styles</u> (2nd ed.). Gainesville, FL: Center for Applications of Psychological Type, Inc.

Levin, M. (1994). <u>Roll of thunder, hear my cry</u>. Westminster, CA: Teacher Created Materials.

Marland, S. (1972). <u>Education of the gifted and talented. Report to Congress of the United States by the U.S. Commissioner of Education</u>. Washington, DC: U.S. Government Printing Office.

Myers, I., & Myers, P. (1980). <u>Gifts differing</u>. Palo Alto, CA: Consulting Psychologists Press, Inc.

<u>National Excellence: A case for developing America's talent</u>. (1991). Washington, DC: U.S. Department of Education.

Onion, S. (1993). <u>A cricket in Times Square</u>. Westminster, CA: Teacher Created Materials.

Osborn A. (1963). <u>Applied imagination</u>. New York: Scribner's.

Parnes, S. (1967). <u>Creative behavior guidebook</u>. New York: Charles Scribner's Sons.

Purkey, W. W. (1970). <u>Self-concept and school achievement</u>. Englewood Cliffs, NJ: Prentice-Hall.

Reis, S., Burns, D., & Renzulli, J. (1993). <u>Curriculum compacting: The complete guide to modifying the regular curriculum for high ability students</u>. Mansfield Center, CN: Creative Learning Press, Inc.

Renzulli, J. (1977). <u>The enrichment triad model: A guide for developing defensible programs for the gifted and talented</u>. Mansfield Center, CT: Creative Learning Press.

Renzulli, J. S., & Reis, S. (1994). Research related to the schoolwide enrichment triad model. <u>Gifted Child Quarterly, 38</u>(1), 7–17.

Rimm, S. B. (1986). <u>Underachievement syndrome causes and cures</u>. Watertown, WI: Apple Publishing.

Sanders, N. (1966). <u>Classroom questions</u>. New York: Harper & Row.

Stanley, J. C. (1991). An academic model for educating the mathematically talented. <u>Gifted Child Quarterly, 35</u>(1), 36–41.

Sternberg, R. (1985). <u>Beyond IQ: A triarchic theory of human intelligence</u>. Cambridge, MA: Cambridge University Press.

Strang, R. (1960). <u>Helping your gifted child</u>. New York: Dutton.

Tannenbaum, A. (1994). The IQ controversy and the gifted. <u>The Journal of the California Association for the Gifted 25</u>(5), 8–9.

Taylor, J., & Walford, R. (1978). <u>Simulation in the classroom</u>. Baltimore, MD: Penguin Books.

Terman, L. (1916). <u>The measure of intelligence</u>. Boston: Houghton Mifflin.

Terman, L. (1925). Mental and physical traits of a thousand gifted children. In L. Terman (Ed.), <u>Genetics studies of genius</u> (Vol. I). Stanford, CA: Stanford University Press.

Torrance, E. P. (1966). <u>Torrance tests of creative thinking: Norms-technical manual</u>. Princeton, NJ: Personnel Press.

Treffinger, D. J., & Isaksen, S. G. (1992). <u>Creative problem solving: An introduction</u>. Sarasota, FL: Center for Creative Learning.

Webb, J., Meckstroth, E., & Tolan, S. (1982). <u>Guiding the gifted child</u>. Columbus, OH: Ohio Psychology Publishing Company.

White, E. B. (1952). Charlotte's web. New York: HarperCollins.

Whitmore, J. R. (1980). <u>Giftedness, conflict, and underachievement</u>. Boston, MA: Allyn and Bacon.

Whitmore, J. R. (1981). Gifted children with handicapping conditions: A new frontier. <u>Exceptional Children, 48</u>(2), 106–114.

Whitmore, J. R. (1986, September). Underachieving gifted. <u>Gifted Children Monthly</u>, 22-23.

Wilkinson, S. C. (1993). WISC-R profiles of children with superior intellectual ability. <u>Gifted Child Quarterly, 37</u>(2), 84–91.

Witty, P. (1940). Some considerations in the education of gifted children. <u>Educational Administration and Supervision, 26</u>, 512–521.

Teacher Created Materials Reference List

TCM 419 A Cricket in Times Square Literature Unit

TCM 434 A Christmas Carol Literature Unit

TCM 525 Where the Wild Things Are Literature Unit

TCM 439 Roll of Thunder, Hear My Cry Literature Unit

TCM 297 Thematic Unit-Ancient Greece

TCM 018 Masterpiece of the Month

TCM 496 Focus on Inventors

TCM 607 Interdisciplinary Unit: Native Americans

TCM 483 Geography Simulations